Real Writing

One Teacher's Journey

By D.L. Smith

Printed in the United States of America

ISBN 978-1-7326621-5-5

Introduction

My mom was the first one to point out the pendulum in education to me. She ran a pullout reading program in a rural farm town. She would prompt, assess, guide and bribe until students were reading at grade level and on-track for success. I was jealous each year when the 'prizes' for her system of external motivation arrived from UPS. Rainbow-colored pencils, rings made of flavorful lollipops, spangled bracelets that clattered together as students walked down the hallway and paddleballs to test the most agile of wrist were the incentives for progressing through the reading levels. The prize station was an ever-present assortment for motivation in the corner of the room. It shouldn't have worked, but it did because she knew the families and found what worked for each student. Mother's classroom was small and cozy and filled with books and energy. The reading kits weren't enough on their own, but implementation by a teacher who cared made them work. This is what teachers do; we figure out how to work around the shortcomings of the programs in place and help students learn. We often do so in a system that can be distracting if we don't stay focused on what truly matters: students' progress as measured through a balanced system that recognizes the need for both basic skills and an understanding of the Gestalt. The real child walks in the classroom door. Even if a bouncy ball is what catches her interest, the incentive to learn can be internalized with the teacher as the catalyst. External rewards such as praise and success and even lollipops can be internalized to create self-motivated learners.

The need for balance in teaching has always existed as policies swing back and forth. In literacy we swing from whole language to back-to-basics and what most teachers understand intuitively is that basics and the big picture are necessary, and learning occurs when both are incorporated in lessons. Students learn the process of turning marks into meaning; and those words have the potential to be life-changing. Anyone who learns through reading or contemplates history, science or literature knows that literacy is key. There is power in the written word. It matters. This is the basis for Real Writing on an existential level—beyond the classroom and the preparation of teachers and the learning of students in the real world. Writing matters. Bringing writing into the classroom is a way to advance learning for all students and provide students with a way to learn.

Writing is important because, as Jeff Zentner states in Goodbye Days, "memory is a good editor". Students focus in on what relates to their worlds. We remember stories and impressions and certain days but many are blurs. I can still do a line-dance I was taught in sixth grade, but I can't tell you the parts of the endocrine system even though I memorized that ten years later in college. Writing in the classroom is important because memory is not enough to rely upon when conducting a lab or listening to a lecture or keeping track of your finances or diet. In the classroom writing can be honed and developed for real-world usage.

If students can explain a difficult concept in writing, then they understand it. In the last three years I wrote over half a million words. Most of it is journals and class plans, and notes on meetings. There is one steamy romance novel undergoing revisions and another 'wolf' novel and memoirs too. What I have figured out over the course of all this practice writing is that it is a great way to learn. Of course, I knew this as a literacy professor, but I didn't understand to what extent until I practiced writing with the same intensity that I used to practice reading. Malcolm Gladwell tells us that it takes 10,000 hours of focused practice to become an expert. If that is true, then I can claim to be an expert reader and expert-ish on writing. Notice I didn't claim to be an 'expert writer'? I am improving through the process of editing and revision. If students become self-motivated learners who infer new meaning through writing, then the level of learning can be greatly increased. I have switched to a focus on writing because the benefits for the Gestalt are endless.

As a professor and parent, I learn through reading constantly, but I approached literacy for too many years as a receiver rather than a giver or a creator. I read texts and signs and updates about the weather and reading keeps me connected and alive. Literally. I read the labels on foods and I follow directions that provide me with basic protections. Reading is a powerful tool, but it is passive until used as a springboard for writing, discussions, reflection and action. No matter how quietly the class sits there and stares at the page you just can't know exactly what is going on in the brain without words—spoken or written.

Writing is a record of our thinking, sometimes revised and often considering audience, but a real record even if edited. The exact process in the brain, when reading and writing, is difficult to analyze. You can track it with running records and reading logs and stream-of-consciousness writing. Students learn through communication or action, but writing is a focus that provides a clear record. Writing provides an authentic measurement for learning in any subject area. It provides the opportunity to capture thoughts. These thoughts can be edited and polished or rough and even harmful; writing is a chance to learn and reflect about whatever topic we choose to explore. So, we write to capture moments or thoughts or to learn. We often start with the personal connection in writing so that learning of the content is increased through the process of writing about prior experiences.

What is Real Writing?

Real Writing is a combination of using writing for learning and Real Talk, which is an approach to teaching developed by Dr. Paul Hernandez that focuses on bringing 'real' moments into the classroom. Real Talk is defined as instructor-led discussions focused on a series of broad engaging themes that motivate student-oriented outcomes. These are created and shared to establish connections, understanding, trust, empathy, and caring for one another. The express purpose of Real Talk is to connect with students, build rapport, and gain insight into students' terministic screen. (Hernandez, 2015)

The significance of learning through writing is real. Organizing critical thinking on paper is how we demonstrate effective communication skills. If we believe that improving critical thinking is a goal for classroom teachers, then the need to teach writing is evident. The goal of progress is important whether we focus in on the details or we question the meaning of life. Each individual determines for themselves what priorities to set just as each teacher must determine their focus. We all find our own path and reflection is a powerful tool for the task. Reflection through writing allows students to demonstrate their critical thinking skills and explore how the content of your class fits into their own lives. One way to make lessons relevant is to provide choices and time for students to make the connections to their own lives. Real Writing is one option for encouraging this in the classroom. It isn't the only option and enacting lessons based on what we believe to be the methods that work for our students is more complex than embracing one more strategy, but writing is a way to learn that is available. All it takes is pencil and paper. This book explores the ways to use writing as a tool for teaching and learning in any content area classroom.

Each chapter is organized so that it starts with an overview of what is explored. The existential question to consider is introduced so that connections can be maximized. The questions and topics that guide this book are as follows:

1. Chapter One: Who are you?
2. Chapter Two: How do we learn?
3. Chapter Three: Who are you to judge?
4. Chapter Four: Diversity matters
5. Chapter Five: Why create your own lessons?
6. Chapter Six: Why make lessons fun and relevant?
7. Chapter Seven: The future of literacy

The main ideas for each chapter are developed with these sections:

Academics for Content

I hesitate to call this section a literature review. One of my favorite studies involved wandering the airport administering a quick reading test to the people waiting for planes. Surprise, surprise, those who were reading when approached scored higher. Much of the research in teaching and learning and literacy boils down to common sense. Teachers are smart people; we don't need to complicate and impress with acronyms and power words any more than a brain surgeon does. But, we do need to agree upon the basics and use research as a guideline.

Question for Reflection:

Each main idea is explored through essential questions for teacher exploration. The best feedback I heard as I shared drafts of this book with friends and colleagues was that parts made them want to tell their stories or respond as they read. Discuss, write, reflect—please share your stories too!

Real Writing Response:

This is my sharing of experiences. The creative, generative side of writing is where I tell my story not as a model of teaching, but as a peek into the reflection process. This is the journey of teaching for me from my first moments in front of a group to my dinner table last night. We learn and teach in most of our interactions so analyzing these experiences provides a platform for learning. By recording positive and negative moments here I hope to demonstrate that we learn from our mistakes and our successes. A colleague told me she hopes to make new mistakes each year. We cannot avoid making mistakes, but we can learn from them and turn them into learning moments.

Learning Moment:

This is a much better label that "lessons learned". That makes me sound like some wise imparter of knowledge. Go forth, young Grasshopper and teach well. In my decades of teaching I continue to grow and learn each year and I hope to continue to do so until my last breath. I never want to be a know-it-all even if I do want to share what I have learned. Classroom learning is discovered through writing and observing and practicing in a supportive environment with safety glasses firmly in place if chemicals are involved. The learning moments throughout this book link with Real Writing and my journey as a teacher. Welcome to one teacher's journey.

**And the Explicit warning: There are a few curse words scattered in the pages because that was the language used during an interview or observation.

Table of Contents

Chapter One

First Impressions

The first years in teaching are a transition period full of learning moments and more raw data than one teacher can compute because the daily task of keeping ahead of the students takes time and an inordinate amount of energy. New teachers find a position that may or may not 'fit' according to personal style and preferences and learn to build a supportive classroom community and figure out their role within the larger community. Learning about school, colleagues, parents, and growing comfortable with the teachers' role is a transition involving complex factors that relate to the question WHO ARE YOU?

In this chapter we explore the question "WHO ARE YOU?" in the classroom with the understanding that the answer is constantly evolving and adapting based on experiences. I start with "Who are you?" because students matter and because I want them to analyze their own community building experiences. The "who are you?" question can be asked and answered in many different ways. 'Who are you as a student?' may elicit a totally different answer than 'Who are you as in terms of music?' Who I am in relation to numeracy or literacy would be polar opposites on my scale and yet I know enough mathematics to get by and I enjoy statistics and the organizational and critical-thinking challenge of math. Each day that we are open to learning more about students is a good day in teaching and learning and this starts by finding out who is in that classroom. The main ideas we will explore in relation to this question are:

- Finding a ‘fit’ and why it matters
- The characteristics of effective teachers
- Building a classroom community
- Getting to know the students

There is something magical about the first day of school. **Tabula Rasa** refers to the blank slate where everyone has a fresh start. We are a compilation of our experiences so none of us truly enters school as a blank slate and yet the potential to create a new experience each year excites many in teaching. I still have difficulties sleeping the night before and I still get psyched to meet the new class each semester. After years of practice I have learned to include these elements to make **a positive first impression in the classroom:**

- A question to awaken students’ curiosity
- The feeling that what they do in your classroom matters
- A sense of community

The question can be theoretical or content-based or general like “who are you?” The topics that are naturally explored at the start of a new learning experience make the link between the students and the content and the course of study. We can’t just tell students that what they do will matter; they have to discover this for themselves by making the links between our classroom and the real world.

There are many lessons to learn in the first years of teaching and we learn more each semester. To be effective teachers we learn to be ourselves in the classroom; we can accomplish this goal by finding our ‘fit’, exploring our experiences, building community and getting to know students each and every semester. Education is a common story we share in all cultures and even in various species. Learning is a common thread and that link is what makes the first impression so important in the classroom. And the next one, and the one after that. Don't worry I understand that the reality of first days is often over-built like so many 'firsts' are. First kiss. First time this or that. You may have many or few. A progressive society teaches the young to find themselves and build an independent world with strong connections. There is much more to the classroom than content.

Discussion Questions for Real Writing Practice:

- Write about a time when first impressions influenced you.
- Explore the topics of who you are as a teacher and how you relate to students.
- What questions will you ask to awaken students' curiosity?
- What kind of community do you consider ideal in the classroom?

**There are discussion questions throughout but not tons of space for writing, so you may want to buy an accompanying notebook. Not to push the chopping of trees—you could take notes in the margins and write small? Or use these to start a discussion…the possibilities are endless.

Academics for Finding a Fit

Each fall thousands of new teachers enter their first positions full of hope and optimism. They arrive with idealism, motivated to make a difference in the lives of the children they teach. Yet their experiences, as discussed by Ness (2001), are often too much to bear for even the most energetic:

> *After two short years the insurmountable challenges have taken their toll: teaching 43 students in one classroom, never having enough desks or textbooks to go around, being sworn at by students, observing countless gang fights, having personal property stolen and vandalized on campus, and teaching through rolling power blackouts. (p. 8)*

The rate of teacher attrition is higher than it is in any other profession (Grant & Gillette, 2006). The numbers are highest in urban school districts, essentially meaning that our urban schools, which need stability, are often revolving doors where teachers spend a few years and then move on to suburban districts or other professions.

Urban attrition rates are high and burnout can occur in any setting, but statistics don't tell the important story of how teachers find their place in the education world. Finding a fit is dependent on who we are and our powers of observation and reflection. According to research, secondary teachers join the profession because they have a passion for their content area. It is a much better reason than "June, July, and August" or for the pay or because I love to read but no one will pay me to do that exclusively.

For some teachers the ideal is a quiet room with no distractions and for others it is outside under the moon and for still others it is in a noisy classroom full of engaged students. If you can't imagine being happy and secure and confident in front of a classroom then classroom teaching is not for you. Maybe parenting or coaching or music lessons one-on-one could be your way to teach but the classroom deserves a unique personality. One who values education and the future and believes that s/he can help shape it and that the way to do that is to teach. My sister is a teacher and my mom was and my husband and friends and extended family members and they are all extremely unique individuals with varying strengths and weaknesses. But they all believe in education and the power it holds for the future. Valuing learning is necessary, but you can be your own special-cupcake brand of awesome if you find the setting that is right for you.

Question for Reflection:

How do you find the right 'fit' for your teaching?

____

____

____

____

____

____

____

____

**I hope you need more space than this. This is provided to remind you that reflecting and discussing your experiences is an excellent path toward growth.

Real Writing Response:

I didn't plan to be a teacher. I was going to be a photographic journalist and live in a loft in New York City and travel the world. Somewhere in my turbulent undergraduate years I declared a teaching major instead. A love of reading books was transferred to a love of learning and progress once I decided to become a teacher. It's just easier to say I went into it because of a love of English. I was “Dr. Snack-Cakes” to my college friends with awareness that earning a doctorate in English was a distant dream. First, I would teach.

We get many first days in teaching. Was my first day as a substitute the very first? In inner-city Flint I turned a lesson on math into sharing my box of Cheezits because the kindergarteners told me they were hungry. Or was my first day when I taught a semester of English in the evenings at Marcos dc Niza High School in Tempe? I didn’t have my own classroom and it wasn’t particularly memorable.

My next ‘first day’ was also my last at Marcos. I replaced a substitute in the Tempe summer school program after the first day of class and was eager to try the workshop approach. We went to the library and students picked out a book to read silently for thirty minutes. We sat in a circle and everyone shared what they read about and learned. Two of the kids had selected children’s books and acted foolish while an administrator observed class. She explained that at summer school there “just isn’t time” because the curriculum is to be covered in half-time. She was kind and found me a position in the office for the summer while I waited for the chance to implement a workshop approach again.

Two months later, August of 1991, in Maricopa, Arizona felt like the official start of my career. Maricopa is a rural school district with three school buildings all sitting on one desolate plot of land in the desert. Two competing bars with crowded parking lots and a run-down grocery store were all that stood out when driving on the highway through town unless you saw the herd of wild horses. Those were an experience more memorable than many of the students who sat in my first classroom.

I was the middle-school reading teacher. I began my first day that year in the same way I began every day for the rest of the year: trying to figure out how to keep thirty seventh-graders under control for fifty minutes when they had nothing to do. First hour was study hall. Classes began at 8:00 a.m. and I watched the clock and waited for 8:50 a.m. like a caged wolf watching Bambi in the field. My management technique has always boiled down to keeping students actively engaged in learning. With no lessons to teach, my lack of preparation for classroom management was glaring.

Despite first hour and some of the worst moments in my teaching career, I persisted and grew in my first position as a full-time teacher. I learned that my principal, Mat, put teachers' lesson-plan books into the trunk on Friday and then spent the weekend on the beach with family and friends. Their little boy was two and laughed as he made sand castles and kicked in the surf. Mat handed plan-books back on Monday morning without ever glancing at the pages. I learned that it is important to take breaks and enjoy family and friends. I learned that teaching is not done alone. I lived and played with people from my school. In many ways, we were family. The community of teachers can be a powerful tool for growth if one is open for learning. I was a sponge. I carpooled with a music teacher, Teri, and listened to her complain. And complain. And complain.

Sometimes she complained for good reason. She "taught" music to kids in a classroom so overcrowded that fire-codes had to be broken. Shoving 78 kids into one classroom and 'teaching' a subject like music K-12 would be overwhelming for the best of us. Teachers can be overworked in negative circumstances until they just can't take it. They explode and quit, like Teri did. So, I learned about a topic that later became my dissertation—attrition in teaching and diverse settings.

After a tough first year I also learned, with the support and help of my fellow teachers and principal, that a middle-school concept is an incredible improvement. We transformed the school from a loud fight-ridden melee into a smoother-running place of learning. We got rid of bells and created block scheduling and a common planning time with the other teachers who taught the same grade-level and started discussing education for our prep time and figured it out together. And separate too. I was learning to be a leader and a reflective teacher.

I carpooled most days in my second year with my two seventh-grade co-teachers. Jed was Jewish and smelled of Gelafish and paste. He taught art and history and the Native-American kids loved how he connected with their culture. Susan taught math and science and was motherly and frazzled and firm in the classroom. Year two got better for all of us. My students came into the classroom asking, "what are we doing today?" excited to learn.

After three years in Maricopa, I had a first day at South Mountain High School in Phoenix and I have had a variety of first-days since. In those first few years I learned how to stage a play despite no drama training beyond dancing in front of the fish-fry crowd at the VFW when I was five-years-old. I learned to plan and teach and reflect. I grew and enjoyed my experience despite a growing realization that middle-school was not for me. I didn't become the statistic I continue to learn about; I followed my dream to teach at the college level and I changed majors because my love of teaching and learning rivals my love of a good book.

Learning Moment:

Finding your fit is a journey and the process involves self-awareness and a willingness to adapt. Your 'fit' in a teaching setting involves determining your strengths and weaknesses with various students and colleagues. You can be effective in one situation or for one student but not in another situation or for other students.

Academics for Effective Teacher Characteristics:

When I ask students each semester to list the characteristics of effective teachers the most common responses include "compassionate, content-area experts, patient, relates well with students" and other terms that are closely aligned with research that lists **organization, clarity, content knowledge and dynamic presence** (2014 Stanford Study) as the top traits of effective teachers. Academic time "on task" is maximized, effective planner and classroom manager, scaffolding and variety in content and process are the traits in an older study. Even though we have very different experiences most of us recognize that these characteristics are what it takes to reach the most students.

The classroom moments that impact us depend on our own individual learning style and thinking critically about these moments can help us to learn. Students complete this simple chart to start the discussion in my class that focuses on what we can learn through reflecting on our own classroom experiences:

Classroom Moments....

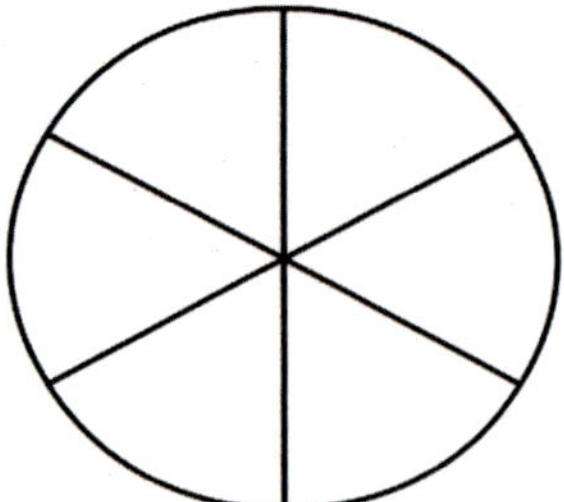

What can we learn from the positives?

Why do the negatives happen?

This activity has a mixed history. I ask students to share their **best and worst** moments in the classroom but the first time it was introduced to me the teacher had us share our positive experiences in math. There were many groans in the room full of literacy specialists.

I do not clarify whether the moments should be as a student, as a teacher or as an observer or what content area needs to be the focus. That is open to the students' interpretation. The responses are mixed as are the examples shared. The questions at the bottom of my form are from a book by **Jaylynne Hutchinson** (1999); she describes a lesson where students create a list of the positives and negative experiences and then examine her critical thinking question:

> *If it is true that as both a student and a teacher you want to create a powerful and positive educational experience called 'schooling,' and if we assume that sitting here today preparing*

to be teachers and educational leaders, we feel pretty much like most individuals who have chosen teaching as their profession, how is it that overwhelmingly our educational experiences fall under the list we labeled as negative school experiences?" (p. x)

For a multitude of reasons, the responses in my classroom were never overwhelmingly negative so I could not phrase the question the same way after my first try. Instead, we explore this mix of positive and negative experiences because critically examining beliefs and practices and relating these to the research and to their own motivation for classroom teaching is a clear route to improvement in the classroom.

Question for Reflection:

What classroom moments have had an impact on you? (or What can we learn from our experiences?)

____
____
____
____
____
____
____
____
____
____
____
____

**I hope you need more space than this!

**Extra question: How does your personality and style impact your classroom?

Real Writing Response:

Two of my examples for class are published pieces. Edward Silver writes of a teacher whose harsh discipline and "you'll never amount to anything" mantra was an inspiration for him. The other is the story of a science teacher who gives students an 'F' after a lecture and a skeleton of a "Catawampus" is used to teach the lesson that critical thinking and questioning what is presented as 'fact' is important in science. Sometimes I share examples from past students, such as the Kindergarten teacher who put a refrigerator box over the desk of students as a disciplinary measure or the high school math teacher who picked his toes in front of class. The examples I share vary from best to worst depending on the day and the group.

I can relate to Edward Silver's choice of inspirational teacher even though this harsh style would never 'fit' in my repertoire. His teacher was strict and made him want to prove wrong her prediction that he would end up in prison. Mrs. Reuster never told me I would or wouldn't amount to much. I remember very little from her seventh-grade English class beyond counting paragraphs to check the one I would read aloud as we snaked around the room reading paragraph after paragraph from a dry text in monotones. I remember writing "I will not talk in class" fifty times. Then one hundred and then five hundred and then the sentences got more complicated just when I had over a thousand "I will not talk in class" sentences in reserves. I remember getting swats. She was elderly so ‘swats’ is plural because they didn’t sting much and talking in class was worth it in seventh grade. But, maybe all that practice writing that I got assigned was the reason I like to write so much today. Eventually her punishments evolved to include essays on how I would improve my behavior in class and I would ramble on for the allotted number of words. Maybe she was a great influence on me, but she doesn’t make the list when I think of past experiences that shaped my teaching.

For that I consider Dr. Bow-Tie and his passion for Shakespeare and how he brought it alive and made me want to be like him. He engaged my interest because of his story-telling skill and his passion for his subject. I wonder if ‘passion for content area’ should go on my list of characteristics of effective teachers. Two other professors who were extremely passionate about their content areas demonstrate the complexity of identifying characteristics with effective teaching. Dr. Yeats taught Irish poetry. He loved his subject and spoke passionately when analyzing the meaning of poems but made students feel stupid. Whenever anyone in class ventured to share his or her own interpretations they were shot down with a ‘wrong’ and soon no hands went up when he asked questions. Dr. WMAE (White Men are Evil) was also passionate about his content. Some of the content facts were new to me. I learned that new-immigrants have higher self-esteem because they haven’t been beaten down by American culture telling them they aren’t as valuable. I learned about the horrors of ESL students given an IQ test in English and then placed in special education when the scores were low. In this classroom others were shut down and treated to ridicule if they offered any input, especially if they tried to point out that there were exceptions to his skewering of all whites as evil racists. This content that I was eager to learn and explore was complicated by his defensive way of teaching about past wrongs. This didn't deter me from embracing the subject and learning, but I am confident that others shut down. So, passion will not make my list—teaching is too complex to just say we need to be passionate about it.

Even if you consider the complexity of teaching and word your choices carefully, identifying 'characteristics of effective teachers' is not enough to become one. I decided 'inspiring a passion for the content' works a little better—which was true of Dr. Bow-Tie but not the others, even though I do still care very much about race and education and an Irish poem is still my favorite—the teachers didn't inspire that, the content itself did.

While I revered Dr. Bow-Tie who shuffled in each week with a huge Shakespearean tome and a bow-tie and proceeded to lecture from the start of class until the end with no time for discussion or interactions, I also recognize he wasn't a model teacher. I went on to pursue English, in part because he inspired me to love analyzing literature, but Dr. Bow-Tie was not ideal for those who learn best through active participation.

All teachers need to have some common talents. They need to be versatile and know their limitations. They need to be on-the-spot decision-makers who are also willing to reflect and improve. And they need to have big egos. I don't want to overstate it but the role of the ego is ginormous. There, I don't think that was overstated was it? How teachers feel about their abilities is the difference between "Hello and welcome" and "Scram, varmint." If you are confident and secure then you have room to reflect and grow and improve. This takes time to develop and time for nurturing. It is less likely to grow without support and sunshine and positive moments and rest. One commonality that teachers and students share is that we are all more likely to thrive in a positive environment if we feel good about ourselves and those around us.

The ego matters in teaching because we must be able to make our own decisions and maintain autonomy. If we give up our autonomy, then we stop questioning the processes in the classroom and a robot could provide the lesson. Creating a positive environment for a variety of students requires that the teacher be autonomous. You must also truly believe that your content is worthy of students' time.

Learning Moment:

By reading and relating to your experiences you can reflect on your own situation and improve. There isn't one prototype for an excellent teacher. The teachers who can reach students vary significantly but they have this in common: they never stop learning.

Academics behind Community Building

The Dunbar number explains that humans are limited to approximately one hundred and fifty 'stable relationships'. Companies and others who have tried to build on this concept found success in limiting the number of employees in a building to 150 for optimizing the interactions. Our inability to empathize with others is a survival mechanism that keeps us from martyrdom, but it necessitates questioning our classroom interactions. The research to support community building comes from psychology, education, medicine and sociology but none explains how teachers who have family and friends and lives of their own are to build community with students when limited to one hundred and fifty total 'connections.'

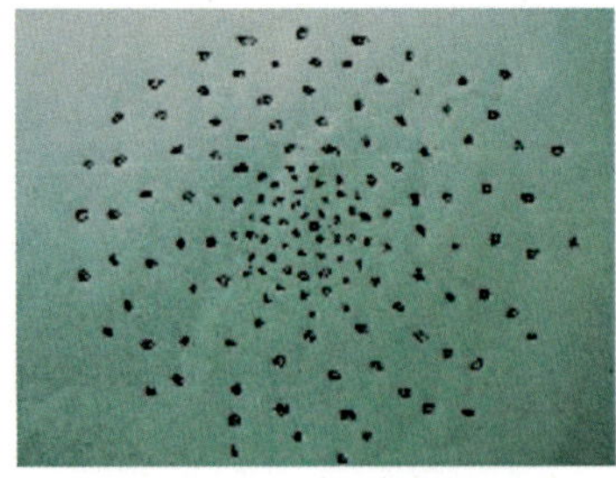

This is how I picture each of us in the middle of our 150+ connections.

One of my favorite stories involves a herd of elephants that existed peacefully in an African region until humans decided to 'cull' the herd. They started with the oldest elephants. What they didn't realize was that the older elephants oversaw the herd and their authority was what stopped younger generations from rampaging chaos. We are talking calves stomped to death and villages invaded. The elder elephants remember a gunshot and avoid the village, but the younger elephants haven't experienced that for themselves and must rely on the community of the herd for their protection and guidance. The medical researchers who link longevity, happiness and health with a supportive community provide enough of an academic reason to build a supportive community but the elephant in the room reminds us that wisdom stops rampaging chaos.

Researchers continue to study community because confusion about what constitutes a healthy community will continue to exist as society changes. We know what happens to the monkey that is raised with no love or comfort. It is not a pretty tale and so the family takes top priority and then the village is there. And that neighborhood includes schools and libraries that value the imparting of knowledge and skills. Building a community starts with a recognition of the support system beyond the classroom door. A healthy respect and awareness of the larger world of students is necessary to build a positive community. Tuning out the outside world and getting in-tune with our own thoughts to learn is difficult for adults, let alone teens and children. A cohesive learning group is essential for creating an environment where distractions are minimized, and learning takes center stage.

Question for Reflection:

How will you build a supportive and healthy classroom community?

____

____

____

____

____

____

____

____

Real Writing Response:

Guns, fights, thugs and teaching Ebonics to a classroom full of inner-city kids when I was a twenty-two year-old white girl with no true diversity preparation could have been a disaster. My student teaching placement worked because I had a strong and supportive mentor and I got to teach *Les Miserable*. To seniors. Mrs. Timm modeled how to run a discussion and how to be respected and she allowed me freedom to teach in a classroom where the discipline wasn't really ever my own. So, I "practiced" teaching but I didn't learn to control a classroom. The seniors wanted to please Mrs. Timm so they listened to me and we learned together. The sophomores feared Mrs. Timm and so they listened and learned too. Nothing magical, but we all made some progress academically.

Learning doesn't need to be 'par-tay' and the reasons we remember what we do are complex but creating an atmosphere where students are welcomed and willing to take risks is an important undertaking for teachers. Community depends upon who we are as people and who our students are and thus it adapts to circumstances and outside situations. People with their own complex histories walk in the door of the classroom. The community built changes based on grade-levels and respect and factors like mood and illness and the time and day of the week. I've taught classes around lunch time for enough years to understand the importance of food and don't even notice the revolving door. It's cool. Students know when to slip in and out appropriately so as not to disrupt the learning of the others in the room. Why? Because they are going to be teachers. They are paying attention to the details and analyzing and listening because they care. Some more than others, I know this. Some days more than others, I understand. A community is built upon mutual understanding. At the high school level I was able to build it with respect, fiestas, cooperative learning, soccer, car-washes, Wilderness Club and too many other factors to mention. Community building starts on day one and is built with each interaction in the classroom.

Community is complicated because formal and informal are both perfectly viable options for teaching. Professional and unprofessional are not; making sure your conduct is professional depends on circumstances. Handholding is less encouraged as students' progress through the levels from preschool to university graduates. Swearing isn't seen as acceptable unless adults are the only ones in the room and even then only if it somehow relates to or enhances the lesson. My son came home recently and let me know his APUSH teacher said “damn”. Twice. I reminded him that my favorite word at the moment is “assholery” and he promised to keep it in perspective. Being real doesn’t mean showing up for work in your pajamas or yoga pants any more than being professional means you need to be uncomfortable. Finding the balance and what works for your situation is a constant variable in creating community.

Over-sharing comes in various forms. The teacher who talks too much or too personally crosses a line that is difficult to draw in a community that cares for all its members. I can think of no reason for my graduate class to have sat around crying as we talked about teaching Harry Potter. We didn’t actually hold hands and sing “Kum Ba Yah” but that is how I describe it because it crossed a line for me. It was too much sharing of personal information, unrelated to the content of the class. One ESL student’s warmth and responsible nature had me hopeful for her future, but I still couldn’t open my wallet when she asked me to help her pay bills. Finding your balance between being “real” and “over-sharing” is difficult when communication lines are open. Teachers are not friends, counselors, parents or protectors but community means we sometimes take on roles that overlap and require balance.

Students must be free to take risks if learning is to occur. A classroom community can lead to anticipation or aversion. Sweet is the feeling that thinking and wanting are almost as exciting as getting. This is the part of me that loves to prepare and plan and imagine. The dreamer and the organizer, and Thursday is my favorite night of the week because it is almost the weekend. Not quite, but looming. Sour are the delays and the uncertainty that the waiting can awaken. Will they like me? Will we connect and bond or will disruptions color the day? At the most basic level what I hope for on any given school day is an understanding that the content matters. What that takes is consensus on why we are there and what it will take to be successful in that setting. Agreement that each person present is valued builds community. Setting goals and understanding motivation helps to create an environment where you and students thrive. From setting the thermostat in your classroom to the hardness of the chairs to the difficulty of the assignment and the pressure for grades there are many factors to consider that directly and indirectly impact classroom community.

Learning Moment:

Teaching and learning isn't that difficult when it is one-on-one. Tell that to any parent and they will laugh you into next Tuesday. Guiding and shaping one person is a lifelong endeavor worthy of great care. It's called parenting. As that ratio increases dramatically we adapt and create communities of learners so that we can empathize within the limitations of the classroom setting.

Academics for "Who are your Students?"

What the 'now' generation lacks is experience and wisdom. Just like generation "X" years ago or the "baby-boomers" before them. To some extent we know who teenagers are through research and experiences and developmental phases. We know they are the next generation and will eventually be the ones running our world. Their choices matter to their own lives and the lives of those around them – their community and society as a whole. They are part of a whole, and they are still individuals.

We don't know their connections and networks unless we know them beyond the classroom or through discussions and questions that help us to know who sits in our classrooms. We start with a foundation of knowing about the school and the age-level and the communities represented and we build from there.

We know adolescence is a time of finding fault with authority and questioning. Arguing to figure out where they stand hones reasoning skills and believing the world revolves around them is healthy as teens find their place or forge new paths. Knowing these common traits doesn't mean we know each overly-dramatic individual. Teens are also known to jump to conclusions and the one they jump to with teachers is that we don't really care about them or we don't understand. But we can understand because we all went through those years and we share a commonality that is stronger than our differences.

Teachers who reach out and let students know they care about who students are through interest inventories and icebreakers build rapport. Multiple small-group and whole-class strategies increase comfort levels; as can icebreakers and building anticipation without heightening fears of failure. Thinking through how to greet students prepares teachers for differentiating in their classrooms and reminds us to consider students and classroom situations afresh each day.

Thin-Slicing refers to our ability to make snap judgments and the accuracy of those impressions. While thin-slicing can yield useful information, the positives are offset by the surface-level nature of the knowledge. We learn about our students because thin-slicing is not enough in education. We cannot succeed with something as complicated as learning on the basis of so little information. Sometimes we must judge a situation quickly; this is the first impression. The second chance comes along each day after that as you learn about your students' learning styles and guide them toward developing skills for independence in your content area.

Question for Reflection:

Who are the students in the classroom and how does that impact learning?

____

____

____

____

____

____

____

____

Real Writing Response:

"Bro, I saw this meme" is how my adolescent son starts many of his sentences. Recently he told me about a woman with child-proof locks all over her house because she has a disobedient service dog. "How funny is that? I mean, the dog could think 'I've had it with this family; I'm out' and leave. This dog opens doors." Our conversation wound from freakishly smart dogs to balancing moderation and 'pale blue dot' philosophy and ended when he said he liked to argue. I had noticed. This is a natural phase for teens—arguing for argument's sake. It is natural and positive and trying as hell at times.

After the first day of school this year I asked my sons how they felt about going back. James, a junior and a stellar student, answered in his usual concise manner. "Conflicted." He does not expound unless asked. Ryan, starting eighth grade, went into a more detailed explanation where he compared school to a death sentence with 'prison breaks' being lunch and the weekend a furlough. He also used the phrase "structured torture" in the description. If a teacher asked this question she could quickly learn their attitudes about school and a bit of their personalities. Most middle-school teachers are too smart to ask this question aloud and they take with a grain of salt the terms like 'boring' that kids this age throw around without enough care, but they still find ways to learn about students.

Ryan is more open and James is more private at the moment. This consequence of their personality and developmental phase means they are striving for independence while also needing support, or teenagers. Ryan does well in school despite his dislike and James neglected to tell us recently when he befriended a pot-smoking man in the woods. "Those were cigarettes Ryan," was his response. They are two of the most complex beings ever and guiding them is important. Teens are sometimes rude, sometimes smelly and sometimes their smile and stories and kindness can warm your heart. Trying to love 150+ of them is close to impossible unless teachers think of them collectively as the future. Which they are.

The need to learn about individual students is why I have started every class I have ever taught, save one, with a **get-to-know** activity. The one exception was a seminar for student teachers at Montana State University and I still cite my failure to start the class with an ice-breaker as the reason that it went poorly. The students in the course were supposed to come to the seminar to discuss their experiences and the discussions fell flat. The student teachers didn't know each other or me and they never felt comfortable enough to ask questions or add their stories to the discussion. Luckily the class was short-lived and never again have I asked students to participate without first easing their tension by building a classroom climate where students are willing to take risks.

This is why teachers who feel autonomy are more successful. I learned from my failure in Tempe that observed lessons should be structured more than a Writing Workshop. I learned from my failure in Montana how to get-to-know university student-teachers. By the time I interviewed for a position at the university level I was confident enough to use a game for my observed lesson. I knew my audience and that classroom management at the college-level is different and I knew the value of finding a fit. Dr. Wolfe watched that lesson and gave me another chance to learn in a different setting. What more could we ask from a teacher? She saw my potential for growth and a new student/teacher willing to take chances. How will you make sure you do the same?

Learning Moment:

Turn Around is a positive option for adding to a discussion as long as the listening was active. Yes, active listening sounds oxymoronish (new word—what do you think?) but it is a conversation habit worthy of the classroom. Stating what you heard allows you to expand upon students' ideas in a way that relates directly to their situations. It is an awesome tool for the classroom if the students and the teachers are listening. To be a student of the classroom we embrace the idea that we learn as much from our students as we teach them. Not about our content, that is our expertise;

our reason we get to be in charge in the classroom. We learn about the students and their processes and progress in the classroom. All I do is tell my story and listen when students tell theirs. Gloria Steinem writes that if you listen to an audience it can become your partner. The same is true in the classroom. If we truly listen to students, they can tell us what they don't know and want to know, and we can learn together.

Chapter Two: How do we learn?

"We think it through" works to a growing extent as children develop into young adults. Yes, guidance when young and when trying new tasks is needed. We learn through positivity and patience with a balancing hand when steadying the bike or slowing down the toddler or teen racing down the drive. In the classroom the three elements that sync to allow learning are the student, the content, and the context. In literacy, this is the triadic model and the elements are the reader, the text and the context, but these need to be updated to reflect that 'text' does not automatically refer to pages in a textbook. Literacy is about communication and there are multiple modes of both.

The broader perspective of how we learn relates closely to literacy and communication. In the Triadic Model each element is given a full side. The teacher and classroom fit into the "context" but overlap with the "students" and the "text" in such a way that comprehension is impacted. The impact can be positive, in which case learning occurs. Or it can be negative, in which case learning is delayed until additional support is provided. The triadic model when used to answer the question of 'how we learn' goes a long way toward explaining how the classroom can be structured to increase student learning. Increase communication input and output.

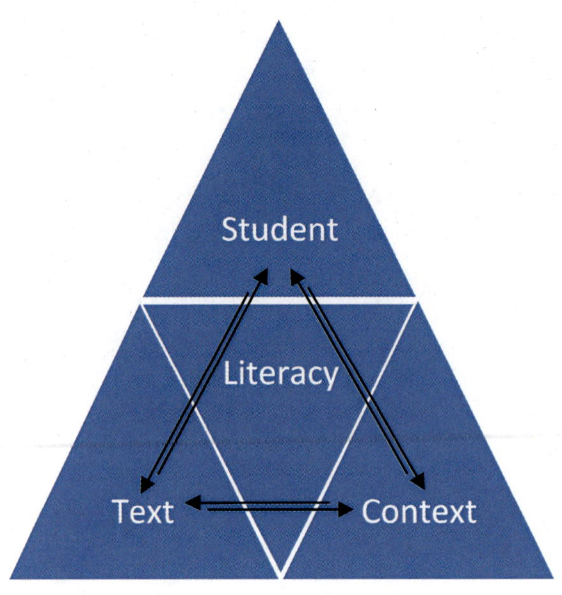

Context:

A student can read $e=mc^2$ and not understand the concept even after it was 'taught'. The letters stand for energy = mass x the speed of light in a vacuum squared. The complex process of creating meaning involves interaction between the reader and the text and the context in each literacy situation. This interaction element means that we are all in a certain situation when we encounter text and it matters. If Einstein sat in the car while I was driving in a snow storm and tried to explain the theory of relativity, then I would fail to understand him. I am too nervous to learn about more than road conditions while driving in a storm.

Student:

Learners use visualization, connection, questioning, inference, evaluation, analysis and self-monitor their learning when they read. **Proficient Readers** (Tovani, 2004) know how to tune-in and comprehend if they can relate their prior knowledge to the text and communicate that understanding. Writing helps students to communicate understanding and to communicate the depth of that comprehension. Spouting off the formula for $e=mc^2$ does not actually denote any depth of understanding. It means we can plug in the numbers but not that we understand energy in its various forms. Who can understand light and the sun without experiencing it? Proficient communicators and scholars and poets and our experiences all vary based on how we learn. But, what we do know is that proficiency in learning increases it and the proficient readers and writers practice it often. This interaction element means that we are all individuals within that context and learn differently based on our experiences and capacities. If Einstein sat in my car I wouldn't even ask him about the theory of relativity. I would ask him what it was like to have inspirational ideas in a time when they were not widely understood. I would ask him to tell me stories of his life. If I got to choose the setting, we would be sitting around a campfire too since that is a nice place to talk; I would learn more about relativity this way too if he really wants to explain it.

Text:

The 'message' is squiggles on a page and we make them into meaningful concepts in reading. The 'text' we choose to present in the classroom varies depending on context and students. The format matters because we know that students learn in a variety of ways. This interaction element means that we face an important decision when we determine text and how it is presented. The classroom is your context and the elements you combine are theories of relative importance relating to learning. We aren't likely to read $e=mc^2$ around the campfire or in the middle of a snowstorm, so this is our chance to select the content of learning to a large extent. What message is selected will influence the learning too.

To explore literacy and the foundational links with learning and communication this chapter explores how these topics relate to how we learn:

- learning theories
- differentiation
- the foundations of literacy
- inquiry-based learning

Discussion Questions for Real Writing Practice:

- Write about a time when differentiated instruction influenced you.
- Explore the topic of how literacy relates to your classroom.
- What choices will you provide to support the various learning styles in your classroom?
- What kind of writing do you consider necessary as a _________________ (fill in a top position in your field…)?

Page for Notes:

Academics of Learning "Theories"

Howard Gardner said, "Discover your difference—the asynchrony with which you have been blessed or cursed—and make the most of it." Howard Gardner's theory started off identifying six ways of demonstrating intelligence, then seven, then eight; some of the charts now show ten. Chickering and Gamson put forth seven principles of effective teaching; one is "Good Practice Respects Diverse Talents and Ways of Learning." Students bring their own talents and styles to the classroom. Brilliant students in a discussion might be lost in a lab or studio; students with hands-on experience may not understand the theory until the connections are made clear. Students need opportunities to show their talents and learn in ways that work for them. Then they can be guided or pushed, depending on the students' learning style, to learn in new ways.

Learning is tricky business. The quote about learning 10% of what you read, 20% of what you hear, 30% of what you see, 70% of what you write about and discuss, 80% of what you experience and 90% of what you teach to another is bandied about in education circles. It is hard to believe that anyone remembers 80% of their experiences; too much of memory is a blur for that one to be accurate and I cannot claim to remember 90% of my class sessions, but the basis for this is reasonable. Schooling that is participatory is valuable. Cognitive, emotional, and environmental influences, as well as prior experience, all play a part in how understanding, or a world view, is acquired or changed and knowledge and skills are retained.

Four Learning Styles that all of us balance:

1. Active. I want to move around and think about the process as I am learning it. I don't want to sit and watch someone else.
2. Passive: I believe I can learn it by watching first and then I can do it myself, if I want.
3. Social: I want to figure it out with the help of friends and we can do it together.
4. Solo: I want to think it through without much instruction or interference from others and then try it before I am graded on my product.

Question for reflection:

How does your learning style impact your classroom teaching? How do your students' learning styles impact their learning?

___

___

___

___

___

___

___

___

Real writing Response:

Most of us learn best when given the time to analyze and communicate. All students need time to think about new concepts. Talent and aptitudes can be increased through practice and patience. Identifying styles is about variety in processes. We cannot tailor instruction for each student in a classroom full of individuals, but we can vary our processes to consider the various learning styles of our students.

Not all teachers can reach all students and some don't even reach most. Mark Barker tutored me in Physics back in high school. He was polite and sat at the kitchen table with me in a quiet home with the sun shining in and birds chirping and I smiled and nodded and didn't ask questions but I learned enough to pass. Why he could teach it to me while the professional could not is about the numbers. One-on-one increases the odds, but not always. Learning is messier than that. Some teachers are simply not aligned with our learning styles. Others are not qualified to pass on information to others in a way that is comprehensible. Tutoring is a *passive, social* style of learning. It is comfortable to those who learn well in one-on-one situation and in small groups and involves talking, writing, and thinking.

Both teachers and students adapt to the situations and the classroom to the extent they are able and share goals. The goal of Stan Holmes, my track and cross-country coach from seventh-grade until senior year, was never clear. He was my history teacher in seventh grade and four girls sat in a giggly cluster around his being. He sat on an unoccupied student desk, with his feet up on the chair. His straggly beard was at odds with the professional attire—a button up shirt and corduroys most days. He talked and probably gave some tests. There were old maps on the walls and dusty bookshelves and about thirty sweaty hormonal students who chose their own seats. The jocks took up the back row and laughed with Stan in conspiratorial ways when Mark Barker peed his seat.** As one of the giggly girls, I blushed and looked away. The other gigglers and I spent the entirety of seventh-grade history trying to write on the teacher with a pen. I may not remember any history lessons, but I was the only one to leave a blue mark across his arm. A middle-school classroom is a confusing mix of *solo, social, active, and passive* at times.

Being held down by the jocks and having a permanent-marker moustache drawn on my face was a story I repeated with a laugh. It was *active.* I also repeated a story about how my father fired Stan Holmes as a little-league coach for the VFW. The repeating of stories is *social* when told. He prompted a group of seven-year-olds to call the other coach a 'witch' and heckle her players. They may not have wanted to, but pressure from an authority figure can lead us to adapt a *passive* style and an adult (my dad in this case) must step in and protect children. The worst infraction was when Stan offered to share a blanket with me when I was still in middle school. A spring meet turned snowy and cold while I shivered in skimpy running clothes until a friend loaned me a big fuzzy blanket. Stan offered to take the blanket as I ran my mile event. When I won the race the 'prize' was an open blanket to share. Fortunately, I didn't have to know seventh-grade history to know to reject that one. I learned that lesson *socially* and probably *solo* too. How we learn is complicated by the lesson. Tutoring is an excellent option in some school settings, but no one should get that kind of tutoring at school. Unfortunately, that was not a story I told until I heard he was arrested for child pornography.

My example is extreme, but we all deal with truly terrible teachers from time to time. In schools we tend to fire those who are incompetent or immoral. Mr. Lockjaw the gym teacher was fired for not filling out paperwork for concussions. He taught health with a paunch and a yearning for the couch. His lessons were *active* but injurious. Mr. Welt was fired from his principalship for having an affair with a students' mother, during the school day, when he was supposed to be in the office. I believe we can classify that one as *social* and leave it alone. Mrs. Wagg, a fellow ESL teacher in Phoenix, was known as a "transfer for disciplinary reasons" even before she pulled over the van she was driving on the way to the zoo and repeatedly struck a student (Edward) with her purse. I believed Edward *actively* learned not to talk about a woman's wig in a *social* situation. So, he actively learned to be *passive*. As an immigrant he didn't trust police to stick with the assault issue. Edward was fine, and the story seemed to mostly revolve around the fact that her wig fell off for the students who treated it like a joke as we enjoyed our field trip.

Another PE teacher yells at kids that he is going to "put your god-damn phone in the trash and you-just-see-if-I-don't" on an overheard tirade. The context of phones with cameras in locker rooms is not lost on me. We all have lessons to learn and styles that work for us alone. In this case I will be *passive* and *solo* but alert. I have not the power to pass judgment without more information at times. As long as we are not passive when students' health and welfare is at stake the choice of teaching style is up to us. For some this means punish for the least infraction because a 'tight ship' matters. Go for it. For some this means students walking in mumbling "motherfucka" as they listen to their Beats. If you are comfortable in that setting, okay. Except in the case of the truly incompetent or evil, most of us can adapt to the classroom and align our goals for learning and progress.

***I am happy to report Mark Barker is happy and healthy while Mr. Holmes is in prison, so karma worked her magic. Also, there are fewer 'bad' students and teachers out there than the media, and this chapter,* *indicate so I apologize for this litany of horrors. It is a good reminder for me that we learn best in metaphorical sunshine.*

Learning Moment:

Some lessons must be relearned each year because children change. Ta-da. The basis for child development is that we accept that there is room for growth. Knowing a student's learning style or the main ones in your classroom can lead to increased learning. Utilizing a variety of methods that develop students' abilities means we are considering learning styles in our classroom. The goal isn't to meet the learning style of the teacher or the student. The goal is to develop learners who excel in all the styles because we need them all in various situations, depending on the content of the lesson.

The Academics of Differentiation

Back in Black, a classic AC/DC song circa 1984, is the song I most associate with team and teen spirit. The rocking beat was played at almost every sporting event I attended from seventh grade until senior year. This song was played on the bus to away games and the sing-along was raucous. We warmed up to it and cheered in the bleachers or on the home-court. On a boom box, the bigger the louder, these words were heard:

> *Forget the hearse 'cause I never die*
> *I got nine lives*
> *Cat's eyes*
> *Abusin' every one of them and running wild*

We believed ourselves invincible and unique. Parents seemed like creatures from another world. Teachers were sometimes monsters and sometimes doofuses but they rarely had impact on our lives after elementary school. I did not see teachers as people with their own stories, despite my mother's link.

Each student wants to hear a story that is relevant and interesting to them. Differentiation requires that we cut through the barriers that separate students from learning in our classrooms. We create circumstances and assignments that meet the learning needs of as many students as possible. What this means practically is that using a variety of methods supports students in learning and prepares them for multiple configurations of interaction. Differentiate does not mean that we track students or that we set lower expectations or that we cater to learning styles to the point that students don't develop other methods of learning. The goal is still an independent, well-rounded thinker in most classrooms. Differentiating means:

- In science: change during development to serve a specific function. (Science tops the list for Google. Is Google biased? Yes or no?)
- In English: the act or process of differentiating. (gee thanks, dictionary… thesaurus is better: distinguishing, discerning, separating).
- In Social Studies: Takes to education link (History: still takes to education links.)
- In math: The essence of calculus; the top article seems to equate derivative and differentiate. I don't think the author understood the definition of differentiate. This could create a misunderstanding.
- In Visual arts: Takes to education links with no 'visual' preference beyond videos at top.

- Product differentiation: branding and marketing term. How does the seller distinguish itself on the shelf?
- In ______________________________: where else do we use the term "differentiate?"
- In education: Tailoring instruction to individual needs.
- How does this term relate to you?

We know that differentiation works (studies, recent). We even know many ways to make it possible, such as project-based learning and programs that coach and measure progress in multiple settings. What we still must figure out each semester is—

Question for Reflection:

How to teach a wide range of students in one classroom?

____

____

____

____

____

____

____

Real Writing Response:

China was a sweet young lady in my college classroom. In this class, we played multiple competitive games involving speedy thinking and varying degrees of collaboration. Americans like competition. Look at the money and attention we lavish on our sports stars. She is right that second-language learners are likely to feel intimidated and slow in this setting; it is still OK to introduce competition in the classroom. We do every time we select a Valedictorian. We can no more ban a competitive spirit than ignore the stress that too much academic competition places on our children.

So, please be critical of those who critique too. I respectfully disagree that competition for thinking quickly and expressing it in a way beyond stating it in unison is a harmful practice in the classroom. We do not need to develop automatons. We need to develop people who excel in all areas needed by communities everywhere. Timid and quiet fits into all classrooms and critique is generally welcomed without defensiveness but be careful that in accepting critique you don't water yourself down to predictable. Don't let routine stymie lessons that deserve attention. If a workshop approach doesn't fit, ask why? If a game is worth playing, ask why? The 'why' can help to develop well-rounded learners. If all you want is an ice-skater, then train and train and train and hope for talent. A well-rounded citizen must learn more than not to speak out of turn and to excel on standardized tests. How do we teach each other to compete nicely if we never play a game? How do we teach tactics and maneuvers for success if we don't understand what matters? Revolutions need leaders, as does the world. To extend our reach with teaching requires that we consider feedback in the spirit of learning and we consider the source.

We know our reach. Not as good as some countries but still producing leaders in technology and entertainment and research and more. Politics, not so much right at the moment. We are not as careful to be equal as Denmark and Holland but making progress. Not as quick to cut off options as many countries. We respect that childhood is about more than academics. We don't rush learning to cram more in because the depth of learning is more important than the breadth at a certain point. Our society needs people who are excellent communicators to lead but also to follow. To trust. And to listen to the feedback of students while balancing that with our own assessment of their needs and the needs of society.

A train went off the tracks recently in the state of Washington. Three people were killed and many more were wounded. It is a common story in our country. Guns and the war on terror are sometimes the details. This time it was Amtrak and accident. Those who build our rails and engineer the tracks should be the detail-oriented people of the world who get it right and check it twice before allowing people on board. The experts. I want everyone to find their expertise based upon talent and time. We can learn cooperation and competition within the same classroom and critique them both. That is the power of the education system in the right setting. We are far from the greatest education system in the world. That is okay if we continue to grow and learn and improve.

How to differentiate:

- Sometimes directly… ask students, "How does this relate to you?" and "what can you learn from this lesson?"
- Sometimes letting the student think it is her own idea.
- Professor: What do you think you can work on?
- Student: My voice projection?
- Professor: Yes, that is right! Your presence in the classroom will need magnified a bit without becoming loud. Fill those shoes and step into the role without posing. If your voice is quiet then use a microphone. If you don't know what to say then listen and respond.

> You don't have to fit a certain 'type' to be a teacher but you do need the confidence to own the classroom and if you can't, then another role is necessary until you can. *Rewind. Build confidence. State it kindly. Feedback requires time to think if it is to be valuable.*

I have students who need to work on voice projection and eye contact for interactions. But, if this is a cultural or generational trait then I don't want to step on shoes. I want to differentiate. I connect differentiation with a teacher's ability to look up and notice and be natural and connect the lesson to the student. Differentiate may mean something different for China.

Learning Moment:

Differentiating is encouraged in both method and content until the student is deemed capable of making independent decisions. At that time the student takes more responsibility for self-monitoring and accommodating for learning. Advocating for children requires understanding their needs. Differentiation is about using both ears and voice and preparing future generations to do the same in a society that values difference.

Academic Background for Literacy: Research Summary

Literacy is a complex process that has been researched upside-down and backwards until we think we know what works. We all learn literacy through our own individual circumstances, but generalizations are necessary in teaching and research provides the foundations for literacy in the content area. Here is the basic summary:

What the research says—

- Read lots
- Variety matters
- Talk about it
- Provide choices
- i +1 (gentle challenge)
- Think and read aloud (model and require participation)
- Include power words
- Make it project-based

The foundations of literacy are the basis for communication in our classrooms. Reading, writing, speaking, and listening are the most common tools for learning and, as such, the language of learning. The foundations of literacy are both simple and complex. At first impression the simplicity of this list is evident and yet, the complex challenge of making it work in the classroom with real students that change each semester is dynamic.

Proficient Reader Research is based on making conscious the processes that good readers utilize as they process new texts. The research confirms that strategies including these processes increase comprehension:

- Visualization
- Prediction
- Questioning
- Connecting to Background Knowledge
- Summarizing/Synthesizing

- Critiquing
- Organizing
- Inferring

Question for Reflection:

How and why are literacy and learning linked for your content area?

____

____

____

____

____

____

____

____

____

**Don't even pretend that communicating and your content area aren't related. The links are evident in everything from PE to learning to play the trombone and more space should be needed to process this important link.

Real Writing Response:

Read Lots

For years I didn't follow this nugget of literacy wisdom. I was busy. I was tired. I wasn't an early reader and my mother's bribery in high school—she paid me to read *Dianetics: The modern science of mental health* by L. Ron Hubbard – didn't have the intended impact. I read thousands of Harlequin Romances and bodice-rippers in those first years. By the time I went to college these were replaced with required texts and Shakespearean plays and textbooks. Some were even memorable, such as *The Color Purple* and *Their Eyes were Watching God.* When I started reading for pleasure again I tried going back but many authors reread as an adult were laughable. Stars and moons, a pink bow-on-top, and gender stereotypes too ridiculous to believe abound. In general, the more you read, the more you learn, except reading the same old tripe doesn't really lead to growth.

In no particular order these are my top ten books at the moment:

1. *Outliers* by Malcolm Gladwell
2. *The Last Lecture* by Randy Pausch
3. *Ten Things I Love about You* by Julia Quinn – a romantic comedy complete with a frisky grandma. I know, I'm a feminist but that doesn't mean romance dies.
4. *Lincoln in the Bardo* by George Saunders
5. *Running with Scissors* by Augusten Boroughs
6. *Their Eyes were Watching God* by Zora Neal Hurston
7. *The Indispensable Calvin and Hobbes* by Bill Watterson
8. *Teacher Man* by Frank McCourt (the audiobook is a treat with his Irish brogue)
9. The Harry Potter Series (book 7 is the best)
10. *The Jungle Book* by Rudyard Kipling

If I wrote the list tomorrow these books may not even make the list just like if you asked me to name my favorite song today it would be *Glorious* by Macklemore and tomorrow it would be *Hallelujah* and the next day it may be the soundtrack of *Les Miserables* and I already want to revise my booklist to include that classic. If your booklist for the classroom consists of textbooks it is time to expand. If you want to think of works of music or art or journals, include those works too. What matters is that we share our literacy, as it relates to our content, with students.

Variety Matters

What you already know here is that the endless variety of materials can lead to 'hit-or-miss' connections in the classroom. Sometimes what you teach is simply listened to in the classroom but all of these are possible outcomes:

- You are ignored (the reasons here can range from the view out the window to a text message buzzing in the bag by a foot. On the floor. Who has noticed?).
- You are laughed at (positive or negative depending on what you shared).
- You are misunderstood (because you didn't explain it clearly or because it was too complicated, or distractions got in the way).
- You are partially understood.
- You are understood.
- You are understood, and the student learns (more like a firefly or lightning than a light-bulb for some).
- The student is annoyed or frustrated or bored.
- The student disagrees.
- The student thinks this is a waste of her time because s/he is going to be a model, not a fill-in-the-blank with the top job in your profession.

- Fill-in-the-blank indefinitely because each individual reaction will inevitably vary.

The variety of reasons that sharing text matters is complicated, but one clear reason is it provides a means of learning and potential engagement. Finding texts that engage a variety of students requires a broad variety of selections.

The difference between reading for fun and reading to learn are substantial and cannot be discounted when considering what text to assign in the classroom. This doesn't mean that we only assign simple texts. It means that we scaffold and teach students to raise their proficiency with multiple types and levels of texts. A variety of reasons to read mean that sometimes it is practice and sometimes learning and sometimes relaxing. Reading for pleasure is a break, an escape, used to relax and unwind. Reading-to-learn can be a pleasure, but it often requires breaks and is as likely to cause a headache as it is to relieve one. Reading-to-learn can become a pleasure when it ceases to be work based on a lack of prior knowledge or basic reading skills. Students can be proficient readers of most texts if provided with the time and incentives necessary. Interest level matters but we slog through enough dry, boring textbooks to know that it isn't required. Stop slogging, by the way, and get better texts. Variety in the classroom doesn't mean beyond your content-area. It means you explore a variety of levels and genres of writing relating to your specific content and you work to find ways to help students learn through text. It is a step towards **independent learning** in your content area.

Talk about it

The importance of conversation as a tool for learning is supported by cooperative learning and literature-circle research. Any suggestion to talk reminds us to monitor **the soundtrack of the classroom.** Be quiet! Too often we talk more than is necessary. Listen instead. Respond. Make dialogue in your classroom meaningful—and don't assume that your own voice takes priority. I recently sat through a speech that wandered from neonatal helicopter units to IGA bags full of cash to a dog biting a parking attendant. A lot of hot-air was expended and the one part that wasn't even mentioned was the reason I was there—the students in the band who sat on the stage and listened too. A music concert should be full of the sound of music. A classroom full of the sounds of students learning will sound different for each of us. What does your classroom sound like? Whose voice is heard and what is it saying? Is it music to your ears? Positive energy? Silence and bursts of cheering can both be golden— this isn't a plea for silence or an excuse to gab; it is a reminder to monitor the soundtrack of your classroom. Some of your students work best in silence while others can concentrate with the hum of the classroom in the background. The comfort-zone that you build in the classroom encourages students to take risks and learn. Learning itself can be uncomfortable—it requires us to expand our minds and admit what we don't know. Talking about it helps.

Provide choices

Choices in the classroom are one way to help students make connections. As a new teacher I wanted to run a reading and writing workshop. Exclusively. Pesky standards, students and the need to cover material got in the way of the spectacular classroom of my dreams. In the real world those matter too. Reading is a way to reconnect with your reasons for teaching and for most secondary teachers that reason is a love of our content area. My department sometimes considers limiting the number of Social Studies or English or Physical Education majors in the teacher preparatory programs because our school systems need STEM teachers or Special Education teachers. The problem with this line of thinking is if I were teaching math I may 'accidentally' let them know that life can still be beautiful without math. But beauty in the world without books? Impossible! The choices can be momentous or minimal as long as the student understands s/he is making her own choices through free will. Free will involves an understanding of the situation and the consequences for learning or not. The links between literacy and the gym can be difficult to understand but the teachers who make those links are the ones who can connect their content to students also. Providing choices and letting some of that responsibility fall to the students is a positive approach that increases learning.

i +1 (gentle challenge)

Teachers are less gentle when the consequences are severe. Stopping a child from stepping into the street without looking both ways is more important than correcting 'seen', as in "I seen it on television." But, both have potential long-term consequences. In my town the consequence of stepping off the curb is a sharp word from the crossing guard. The other consequence is more insidious, but just as important. People view you as inferior because of grammar mistakes. Society equates intelligence and class with dialect too often not to teach students to code switch when appropriate. We also teach that code switching doesn't mean adopting a condescending British accent. It may sound brilliant, but keep it real.

Teachers figure out how to scaffold for learning and present content in ways that are relatable and clear to students. Teachers do not need to tie balloons around little ankles with vocabulary words inside and allow chase scenes in the classroom to disrupt the day to make learning active. Games can be a break from sitting and 'learning' in the traditional classroom but there are better ways. Meeting the challenge is the fun part of learning. Resistance is the most likely result of frustration or boredom. The intricacy in teaching is finding the balance. Learning can happen whether from our mistakes or our successes if time is provided for reflection—success is much preferable, but the lessons can stick either way. A gentle challenge provides the level of difficulty that maximizes learning.

The easiest and most accurate analogy is steps. We learn in steps and when practiced we can take them with fairly large leaps; with fewer connections the height must be lowered. Not to the level of 'a ribbon for participating' that sometimes happens when adults are too busy to take the time to provide genuine feedback. The coaching kind of learning that leads to growth can happen without us noticing (how I learned literacy because I was surrounded by it) to incremental planned steps (like a classroom with supports can operate) to a free-for-all like how we 'learn' about God through spirituality. We never know students' true aptitude until we engage them and get them to consider our subject area and learn with us. They have to take the steps, and we have to provide reasonable support and maintain our own balance. And, provide the opportunity to learn our content.

Think and read aloud (model and require participation)

If the teacher put this visual on the board and provided time for you to read, adequate time and maybe even choices of music with a large variety of options and told you to talk about it and nicely asked you to play it on the trombone, could you read the notes and do it? How about if it were written in Arabic? Or Sanskrit? How about if the teacher played this musical selection and asked you to repeat it? Modeling is often the key to repeating a basic skill. But I still wouldn't be able to read the music without guidance. The process for communicating needs to be broken down so that students can learn. It is not enough to teach students memorization skills or even to ride the bike on their own; students need to be able to communicate and expand their learning.

As of right now, I can barely make a sound on the trombone. I am confident, that provided some time and the model of this piece of music, I could play it eventually. It would take less time if I could ask questions. It would not require that I be able to read this text. So, why teach students to read the text of your content-area? Because repeating what is heard is not enough for learning. A musician must feel the music and read the music and maybe even write music of their own. Not everyone gets to be a rock-star, but no one gets the chance without knowing the basics.

You do not have to be a professional mathematician to teach math, but you do need to be an expert in math. This content expertise from which we teach is what makes us qualified to stand in front of the classroom. And a certificate and passing the 'fingerprint' exam and, yes, I know there is more than content but it is our top criteria as students move to higher-levels of learning. You are the expert in the classroom and modeling the process you use when reading aloud and thinking aloud and even taking notes are all necessary to show students how to learn. Then they need the critical-thinking skills to take that learning beyond. We don't teach so that students reach our level; we teach so they can surpass and expand the knowledge-base. Progress is measured in terms of contributing to the good of the whole. The whole child. The Gestalt. One way to make progress is to lead the way and model for your students. Do not just tell, but show students and lead students to understand how and why your content is worthy of communicating about clearly.

Include power words

My Uncle Geno was an armed robber before I knew him. I don't know the circumstances or the story, except that he was convicted and served time while my aunt waited patiently for her man. We can only judge if we know the story and our versions and perspectives can be skewed depending on our own terministic screen. This is our mask. It is more than a perspective.

"Gestalt' and 'terministic' are my power words. Power words are subjective; not many educators would include words like "gestalt" and "terministic" in a book devoted to literacy but 'terministic' is a word I associate with Real Talk and "Gestalt" is a term I associate with writing. The big-picture relates to Gestalt and terministic is a detail word to indicate that students bring more to the table with them than background.

They bring attitudes and their own power words and current life situations and moods.

Make it project-based

The main ingredient necessary for a project is a real question or problem. As a dedicated do-it-yourselfer I complete many home projects. The current project, put up a new medicine cabinet, has real questions like "how big can the medicine cabinct be?" and "how will I make it solid so it doesn't fall off the wall like the last one did?" These are my real questions for the project that will indeed take an extended time to answer and solve.

The complicating factor with project-based learning is that it is often cooperative and many of us are not skilled in working with others. Group projects only work when the members have roles and understand interdependence for success. Putting up the medicine cabinet on my own is not a difficult task, but if others get involved and have different approaches to the project then the challenge increases.

1. Identify a problem.
    a. Is it real?
    b. Is it important?
2. Break it down
    a. Define it.
    b. Research it.
    c. See if there is an ideal to study—a model for how to change?

3. Brainstorm solutions.
    a. How can we have a positive impact?
    b. What do we control and what don't we control?

Learning Moment:

We know what the research says and what good readers do and at the heart of learning is providing time, support, and a balanced approach. In the end we realize how we learn and what we learn depends on the classroom and the lesson. As teachers, we decide and the assessment system measures.

Academics for Inquiry-Based Learning

Anyone who ever sent an angry text knows that the stages of writing are not always followed just like the stages of learning are not always followed. Both processes are recursive as often as linear and very few march steadily forward or follow the same pattern for different tasks. Some lessons must be relearned multiple times before they stick (mostly the ones relating to communicating clearly and kindly) and some are instantly learned (mostly the ones involving pain). But, no matter the lesson, stages are one way to approach a learning situation if we believe it will be complicated. Like a well-worded question.

The question I asked was "who could explain the connection between inquiry and learning?" and the answer for me was Dr. Paul Hernandez. Introduced briefly earlier, Paul is a TED-talking administrator whose goal is to lead education into a future where those who struggle early on are accepted as the hope for the future. His story is an inspiration and a model for how to solve problems in the world of education. He is a success whose history makes him an Outlier. Except he had advantages too and credits most of those to a loving mother and some other teachers along the way.

The following is from Dr. Hernandez's perspective:

Real Talk for Problem Solving by Dr. Paul Hernandez

(shared as a power point for my Real Writing Cadre grant in 2016)

1. Pretend the subject for the day or week is problem solving. You will begin with a Real Talk for the class as you introduce the subject.
2. In the next few slides you will find my example of a Real Talk but keep in mind that it seems very long when presented in a PowerPoint vs. when you actually give the talk. Length of Real Talks will always vary.
3. **My Real Talk Example:**

Problem Solving is something I did in the streets all the time. But I never realized I was doing it because we didn't call it problem solving. One of the most difficult problem-solving situations I ever encountered was attempting to change my life. I reached a point in my life where I became tired of constantly having to pay fines and deal with the police. I had to ask myself how I kept ending up in bad situations. I wanted money and success. But my problem was how I tried to achieve success and money. I was involved in illegal activities attempting to achieve my goals and this was my major problem. I was taught in the streets that this was the way to succeed. I had never heard or knew anyone from my neighborhood who was successful by being legit and going to school.

Having figured out that my problem was being involved with illegal activities I began to think of a strategy on how to escape deep poverty without being involved in illegal hustles. I decided that my strategy would be to enroll in a community college and see if I could make school work for me.

I hated school in the past but I thought that perhaps I could find a major/subject that I would like and I could find a way to make legitimate money. With all the hustles I was involved in I always wound up losing money by being busted and with legit money I figured that no one would be able to take that from me. I enrolled in a local community college and although I was nervous I was not going to quit.

As I struggled in community college I was fortunate in meeting some professors who were helpful and offered me guidance. With the help they offered me they introduced me to new resources. But most importantly they attempted to connect with me and I felt as if they accepted me as a person. This helped keep me motivated in staying in school because there were many times that I simply wanted to drop out.

As the years rolled by and I stayed in college I stopped getting into bad situations and having to pay expensive fines. As I reflected I realized that things were much better than they had been in the past now that I progressed in school. It wasn't easy to make the change from hustling in the streets to becoming legit and going to school, but I do not regret having made the change in my life.

Note: This is where I transition into problem solving and its connection with school/class/subject matter.

The changes I went through in my life stemmed from problem solving by approaching my life and analyzing why I was spending so much time in turmoil and always ending up "broke".

1. **Connecting with Students:**
   a. What positive or negative examples can you give about problem solving that you have experienced or heard of or can think of? Whether you share a positive or a negative experience, make sure that you always end your example on a positive note.
   b. You want to welcome both personal experiences and their own critical thinking perspectives/comments/questions.
2. **Begin the Curriculum:**
   a. Now that you have established your Real Talk and the students have given their perspectives or examples you begin the required work for your class.
   b. Remember to keep your lessons interesting and diverse along with periodically "dropping" a Real Talk on the class as you feel it is needed.

Question for Reflection:

What is the connection between inquiry or problem-solving and learning?

____

____

____

____

____

Bonus question: If metacognition is thinking about your thinking processes then what is the word for writing about your writing processes? **Scriptocognition.** *Yes, another newly-minted word coined.*

Real Writing Response:

I learn best through writing, so I will process this question through the filter of the writing process.

Planning— Respond to a real-world problem with a real-world solution. Not pie-in-the-sky and sing Kum-by-yah, but real-world is the goal. The route we take will be different for each of us. Any progress is better than none if the problem is overwhelming.

Only go to meetings where there is an agenda. I researched this. It is important.

The same should be true for the classroom. Leaders who value students' time understand the importance of planning. The first step in writing or teaching or starting a project is planning.

Drafting— Raw Writing. This is the basis for real writing. This is the stream of writing that flows without edit or with minimal editing and captures the thoughts as they move toward understanding. Students simply write it down in some format. A map. A pro and con list. A list of possibilities or necessities to make the solution viable. Learn some too. Google it and read a book or an article and shape your response according to your new information. Remember this is just a draft. You can brainstorm even if it is pie-in-the-sky.

Feedback: The beauty of the positive and the justified critique must be tempered whether the reflections are personal or public and only through honest and respected sources should we seek feedback. Dr. M rated me super-high, but it meant far less than Dr. R's honest ratings with written comments and respected shared history. Dr. M supposedly was given a back-water doctorate and did not deserve respect. The further your connection the less the feedback matters. Thus, the feedback of family, friends, and respected colleagues means far more than a distant evaluator. Own the process if you want real feedback and seek respected sources. Read aloud and listen to how it sounds so you can create your own feedback too, especially in the early stages.

Sharing—two heads are better than one is a saying for a reason. Example—the Korean and Columbian pilots who crashed because the co-pilots were too subordinate to speak up. The Korean and Columbian pilots who didn't tune in and listen to their co-pilots because they thought they knew best (Gladwell, 2008). Speak up and listen and truly share ideas and great solutions can happen. This may involve group work or a partner or an outside opinion. Who you share with and how your ideas are presented can matter—so select carefully and state yourself clearly.

Evaluating—occurs throughout. It is how you separate pie-in-the-sky from possible and why some ideas are dismissed while others are embraced. Be sure your evaluating is done fairly and consistently and use it for growth and improvement of the plan and draft and then again after sharing as you or your group move forward.

Revising—also occurs throughout while thinking and researching and sharing if you are working on being clear and listening. Communication skills are important, and writing is one way to communicate. Clarity matters in all the forms, but clarity in writing can improve all communication skills. This means that if you are writing journal-style or stream-of-consciousness more editing and revising are needed. If you are writing after mulling over a problem in your head, then you may need less revising and deleting. This will depend in each case upon the intended audience and purpose of the writing. What makes it real? Who will read it?

Editing—At some point a finished product is required. An answer to the challenging question or a solution to the real-world problem must be formulated and presented. How you express the answer or present the solution determines your success on the project. Can you communicate clearly and demonstrate your learning?

Publishing—in some cases the 'publishing' involves turning it in to a teacher or presenting to class or submitting elsewhere or sharing with a friend. Students learn about audience when sharing the knowledge is a valued stage.

Learning Moment:

Throughout college I wrote out my completed essays in one long-hand draft and then paid Liz's mother to type them for me. I did not own a computer or even a typewriter and I was working in a bar and renting a room in a house shared with Liz, a young single bartending mother. I thought it all out in my head and wrote down organized paragraphs stating my case. I no longer write this way, preferring a stream-of-consciousness style that requires intensive revision and editing. The process of writing is complex and grows with the person. Writing improves problem solving and vice versa. Inquiry is the question we answer when we stare at a blank page and start writing.

Chapter 3: Who are you to judge?

Judging, evaluating, and assessing are all terms that relate to accountability measures in education. For this chapter we will explore assessment as it relates to the collection and analysis of data to inform decision-making in the classroom and the providing of feedback and setting of goals to increase learning. Assessment is the proverbial double-edged sword. You cannot make progress without it, but accountability measures that rank schools, teachers, and students, deeming some 'failing' while others get 'stars' can cause stress and give assessment an undeservedly negative reputation. The double-edge is an apt description of assessment because both sides cut. Critique can slice when it is individualized and specific and provided as a means for improvement. When it feels distant and extraneous to progress it cuts into valuable time. The stakes often seem high and the interruption of teaching by measures that are unused beyond larger accountability issues makes it difficult to see the positives at times.

So, can we assess a math teacher? Absolutely, and, apparently, we can judge professors and presidents too. We all are judged and judging whether we are reading or writing or listening or acting or speaking. The critical aspects of this make it a challenge that is best met with an agreed upon set of standards. Assessments in education are 'standardized', meaning that they align with the standards. Whose standards? Those in the 'academy'. Except leadership, empathy, collaboration, and creativity (to name a few) can't be standardized. Which was the unforeseen problem with the rush to standards-based education. The positives of equalizing expectations come at the expense of artistry and innovation and character because those can't be reduced to numbers. School is about more than academics and thus our measuring of all things 'schooly' with standardized tests is not possible. Standardization is a positive step if implemented with this understanding in place so that we do not mistakenly equate school for life. Dewey's states, "Education isn't preparation for life; education is life." Most of us don't want a standard-issue life; we want more and that requires using good judgment.

When the climate of a school feels pressured or stressed the numbers are likely to indicate that the students there are not achieving comfortably. Suicide rates on one end and violence on the other increase in unhealthily competitive climates or climates that don't increase academic independence for students. Judgment is needed for educators and communities to make competent educational decisions on matters ranging from format to methods to content. We trust communities to make intelligent decisions about education if the individuals and the numbers appear to thrive; the pressures stem from figuring out the best course of action when the individuals and the numbers indicate that the system is not being held accountable for students' learning.

The focus on achievement appears to have gone out-of-control in our culture according to many. Less empathy, lacking leadership skills, a dearth in initiative and questionable collaboration skills are on this path of high-pressured testing, not to mention the health detriments associated with stress and isolation (Abeles, 2015). We need to judge more than students; we need to judge the system when it is failing our students. Standards-based education is not failing our students, but the accountability measures can feel distant and onerous unless teachers remember the true purpose of assessment—the guidance of learning.

A system that uses the data collected to guide students toward progress needs little feedback and even the 'great job' said with heartfelt sincerity and awards such as top-rankings can be viewed as arbitrary because too often we cannot truly evaluate the performance separate from a community. It is the "attaboy" of feedback used for the winning team or the band that performs flawlessly. The judges and measurements are not always fair but there is merit in a show that goes smoothly whether the 'stage' is the classroom or the movies or the performance review. Someone got a "four"? Can you believe it? Yes, we all judge and in doing so we must set priorities.

We are all worthy of judgment; (not in a religious sense, thanks to the law of separation of church and state) but not all judgment is worthy. In the classroom we try to keep our assessments narrowed in on potential and learning. Deserving and not is too often decided based on similar priorities rather than actual merit. The oppressors and the oppressed throughout history have struggled with determining just deserts. What a terrific term, as though a big chocolate sundae with whip cream and a cherry on top, is the equivalent of the pursuit of happiness. Students come to school with disadvantages and advantages based on family background

An oath, like the Hippocratic for doctors, may exemplify how teachers are driven by a sense of right.

A Teacher's Oath:

- *Do no harm*
- *Instill a love of learning*
- *Support and encourage growth as appropriate to students' developmental needs*
- *Provide a safe learning haven*
- *Encourage*

and abilities. Academic abilities are judged while in education we try not to judge background. Separating these is nearly impossible, but the classroom is a safe place for all so that is the aim.

Assessment is as simple as asking a student to stop and be kind and as complex as the teacher learning to be proactive enough to say "PAUSE" loud and clear when a student says, "I don't want to offend anyone…" in the middle of a conversation about a sensitive topic in the classroom. In the movie *Talladega Nights* Ricky Bobby says, "with all due respect" followed by ridiculously rude comments to his boss. We have all spoken in regrettable manners and the teacher anticipated this possibility. The teacher quickly said, "then stop right there and think" and the student slowed down to ensure his words were not offensive. The brilliance of putting a "stop" to the conversation comes from experience and reflection and assessing the situation. That is a teacher move worthy of repeating. The difficult part is the need for critique to make progress and the agreement on priorities for the classroom. The progress we make in learning lessons is related to our ability to process the classroom critically. If we talk about experiences with others and journal and listen, we learn with less repetition of mistakes because we learn from processing classroom experiences. What we consider a 'mistake' depends on our critique of the situation. Honing our abilities to critique others and ourselves fairly takes practice and consideration.

In the classroom it makes sense that we evaluate and judge because that is the path to critical thinking and critical literacy. Doing so in a way that encourages learning is the challenge. We don't ask questions to stir up passions without considering the consequences and all the possible truths. Education utilizes judgment. It is Bloom's top level of cognition; it is the pinnacle of thinking. Yet, we know that our judgment isn't final. It is a building block and the students eventually become the builders. We judge to guide so that the future they build is safe and kind.

Why else do we judge? On a very basic level we judge to survive. Instinctual judging relates to evaluation at the very top of Bloom's taxonomy. Judging is complex enough to include refined skills worthy of development and basic survival mechanisms. What it means to be educated today involves communication skills and computing skills and critical-thinking skills. There is even a bias toward finding those who critique to be more intelligent (Grant, 2016). We judge because smart matters in our evolution; moral reasoning is necessary to consider how to 'do no harm' while setting and measuring progress toward standards based on values shared in society.

Data collection and management are integral to measuring learning; the link with literacy and writing is evident. The goal of education is balance, not an end to assessing or grades, but a story that allows us to connect with students and assign them numbers and the chance to explore the various subjects with fairness and integrity. Not on personal whims until proven capable of making their own academic decisions. That way leads to chaos. Just like the other way leads to automatons. Our path is clearly illuminated by science and the arts alike. The goal of this chapter is to consider how to keep the judgment part of education focused on achievement. The goal of it all is life, liberty, and the pursuit of happiness.

We explore the topic from these angles in chapter three:

- driven by more than data
- valuable feedback and guidance
- critical literacy and
- setting goals

You can see the education system as a race to nowhere or you can see the value in teaching students how to think and explore a liberal education. Or, you can see both sides. The assessment initiatives that call for finding balance are the ones worthy of support; the ones that balance numbers with individual students. This chapter is dedicated to aspects of assessment that overlap heavily with writing and literacy. Judging writing and literacy is impossible to avoid because most measures require the communication skills to express understanding. Figuring out how to assess and keep it real is important to all disciplines and in most critical thinking decisions we make in school.

Discussion Questions for Real Writing Practice:

- How do you maintain a 'continuous improvement' attitude?
- Why design assessments to guide student learning?
- Write about your material selection process for the classroom.
- What, beyond student progress, deserves regular assessment in our schools?

Academics for Driven by more than data:

There was a time when the book *Driven by Data* and the standards movement sucked many educators (myself included) in to believing that data was the key to forward progress in the classroom. The four key principles still weave a magic dance as alluring as time. "Trust the numbers," they whisper.

1. ***Assessment*: Create rigorous interim assessments that provide meaningful data**

The key terms here are generally agreed upon in education. Rigorous is a reminder to keep our expectations high (independent learning) and interim keeps a time limit on how long we go before we measure results and adapt based on progress. Meaningful data to start is appealing as evidenced by the backward design concept. Starting lesson preparation by considering the outcomes expected means teachers are more likely to reach the outcome.

Data is only meaningful if it is used to improve instruction. The teacher who gave her class a pretest on calculators and figured out that over half of the class already knew the information and then proceeded to teach an entire lesson on that same information was not using the data in a meaningful way.

2. ***Analysis*: Examine the results of assessments to identify the causes of both strengths and shortcomings**

This analysis tells us what our students' learning needs are. The balance of finding the strengths along with the shortcomings is paramount to valuing differences and being kind.

In a classroom of twenty-five, if fifteen of the kids already know how to use a calculator, then there has got to be a better way to have the ten students learn it than to make the entire class sit through a fifty minute 'calculator' lecture. This teacher's strength is her sunny smile and her weakness is apparently differentiating.

3. ***Action*: Teach effectively what students most need to learn**

This is our aim. Identifying the needs of students and meeting those is the primary role of education. Our hierarchy of needs mean that care and basic needs must be met before progress is possible. Sleep, food, and safety: the basics of survival are met, and comfort is increased as the alignment between the teachers' skills and the students' needs are aligned.

An effective method for catching up ten students in their calculator usage would be to pair them up and have the students who know the material demonstrate while the learners practice; a game where only the kids who need to learn it can touch the calculator could engage. Or the ten students who need calculator practice could work with the teacher on the skill while the rest test their skills with more advanced problems. Figuring out how to challenge thriving students and support struggling students requires multiple plans with extension activities and adaptations built into the plans. Again, there has got to be a better way than a fifty-minute lecture on calculators.

4. ***Culture*: Create an environment in which data-driven instruction can survive and thrive (Bambrick-Santoya, 2010)**

A system that thrives is a reasonable goal if the system doesn't grow self-important or bloated. Education exists for the betterment of society. A lecture on calculators even when the pretest demonstrates that students know the lesson is not an indictment on the culture of assessment, but it does highlight the challenges. If the data teachers receive isn't used in effective manners than the culture isn't healthy.

The *Driven by Data* principles are so reasonable as to feel innocuous even if the perpetuity of principle four seems self-serving. It is the additional directions and technicalities that hoodwink. Statements such as "analyze the end-goal test (MEAP, ACT, AP, IB tests available online)" clearly place the value on standardizing assessments. The follow-up of "effective data reports collect question-level, standards-level, individual student, and whole class data – the best ones do it on one page per classroom" make it clear that the number is king in a school driven by data.

Overall, teachers trust the numbers and research in education. We tell students "the research says this or that" and expect that the statistics and numbers supporting our words are enough. No student can be boiled down to a number, a score, a grade or a performance review. Data is only as valuable as the decisions it helps teachers to make. Drivers know that 1.0 is a magic number that must be avoided if drinking and then getting behind the wheel. The APA claims 2.0 hours/day of screen time is a reasonable limit. Being driven by more than data does not mean we discount tests and averages and all the wonders of science and measurement. Those are awesome and GO SCIENCE!! Seriously! Valid and reliable data is necessary to determine our best practice and reform the education system. Our schools will best meet the needs of society by considering research and developing students' learning potential in a warm and supportive environment. Not the sterility of a lab, but a classroom. Schools need data in obvious ways, but data is the tip of an iceberg in the scheme of classroom learning.

Question for Reflection:

How can you design assessments that are rigorous, timely, and provide meaningful data and use these to guide instruction that will result in learning?**

____

____

____

____

____

____

____

** A complicated question for a complicated topic

Real Writing Response:

Evaluating students' progress with numbers and grades is important, but less important because those numbers cannot tell me enough. "Enough" data is provided by triangulation. Triangulation is a term used in educational research to indicate that three measurements are taken to increase the validity (accuracy) and reliability (consistency) of the results. Students who can demonstrate understanding in a variety of ways let us know the results are valid and reliable. I am pretty sure that filling in bubbles or blanks is not much of a skill for the real world; standardized testing is not enough.

In my second year of teaching I struggled with management and content but I developed an assessment system that was amazing. By accident, believe me, I'd like to take credit, but this one was a fluke. My students were given a diagnostic assessment that year in September while I was still learning names and building community. I got the results right away. Having been provided with no curriculum beyond boxes of class-sets of YAL novels in my first year, these results fascinated me enough that I made a chart. Each 'skill' in ELA was listed along one side and students' numbers were listed across the top. Gold stars were placed for each skill a student 'mastered' by answering three questions correctly. I placed this poster in the back corner of the room, behind my desk where I believed students would largely ignore it.

Here is a mini-example:

Student/Skill:	Atoll	Gobbler	Sweet	Wanker	Curd
Ability to interact appropriately	★	★	★	★	
Diversity: First- hand knowledge	★		★	★	★
Knowledge of Quantum Mechanics		★			
Knowledge of Literacy			★		
Knowledge of community building		★	★		
Can identify 'good' teaching	★	★	★	★	★

I proceeded to teach mini-lessons and have students practice the skills identified by the assessment. I balanced this instruction with the other literacy skills I deem important and integrated as often as possible. I would teach a lesson on commas and then have students work on the skill in their own writing and then I would create an assessment where students answered three questions. If the student answered all three questions correctly then I placed a new star on the chart. If we were reading *Lord of the Flies* at the time the examples used for questions related to that book too.

After a month or two of this process and getting to know students I started having students who chose to spend their lunch hour in my classroom. I welcomed their company and when they got comfortable they started asking about the chart. Soon, their interest at lunch turned into a crowd of students asking me their student number and how they could earn stars. They begged me to create new assessments, so they could demonstrate their new-found talents in the use of semi-colons, periods, and each 'skill' associated with literacy on the diagnostic assessment.

The 'gold stars' were enough of a reward but I decided to make it more cooperative. We celebrated with small rewards when the entire class mastered a skill. Learning games, a break in the form of a round of 'Seven Up', or a nature walk with the intention of collecting 'adjectives' were some of the rewards I used. And candy and pencils and 'parties' that involved bringing food and listening to music; which enhanced our community spirit still more. Ultimately, we want the reward to be independence and the new skills themselves, but I wasn't even aware that a debate on rewards in education raged. I knew that I was using assessment to guide students' learning in a successful manner and that was the kind of reward that made me want to keep trying in the classroom.

At the end of the year the students retook this assessment and most scored 100%. It didn't mean they were experts at literacy; it meant they learned some skills that would help them be better readers and writers. It meant they were expert bubble-fillers for one day and that may have meant they tried more the next year. Or not, I didn't follow their progress beyond my academic year with them.

I have continued to struggle with assessment despite knocking it out-of-the-park in year two. The more advanced the concept the more difficult it is to measure. The more complex the skill being measured the more complex the assessment process and the measurement necessarily must be. In my classroom I am looking for moral reasoning, positive dispositions, and other factors that are not bubble-fillers or even fill in the blank options. The most valuable feedback I provide comes in the form of one-on-one conferences after I observe a student practice teaching. I am an expert at identifying good teaching and I use this skill to determine if prospective teachers have the pedagogical expertise to practice their craft in the next stage of student teaching. This is an awesome responsibility, but it is shared by host teachers and supervisors and other professors and the state exams and factors beyond my immediate control. This is what we do when we trust an education system to provide and triangulate our data.

Learning Moment:

Dank numerical skills are extremely helpful even if not the pinnacle of the profession. Numbers that are valid and reliable and aligned with what we consider important can tell us what skills to work on next. The rubric is the determining factor in the rigor of any open-ended question and how we develop and evaluate on such a rubric is subjective which means that numbers just can't be enough. It is valuable if the system is pure so let's stick with valid and reliable and understand that defensible is common sensical.

Academics for Valuable Feedback and Guidance

The **first rule** of providing valuable feedback and guidance is to remember that truth is subjective. J.K. Rowling got rejection notices for the Harry Potter series and the first man to say the world is round was laughed at, ostracized, and maybe even stoned to death. (*I fell asleep during that lecture back in high school, so I may not remember the end of the story accurately).* The other first rule is to be prompt, positive, and keep it specific. Feedback that is vague and delivered too late or delivered in an overly harsh manner does not guide students toward development. If you are offering feedback that is not about guidance, then consider the reasons. Worthy praise can be worded to encourage effort and even 'you shouldn't have' can be a valuable message if the goal is to stop further mistakes. Just remember the subjectivity of your feedback.

The **second rule** of providing valuable feedback is that it must be 'doable' to be valuable. People don't like giving speeches. Those who were told to state "I am calm" didn't improve. Those who were told to state "I am excited" did much better (Grant, 2016). Fear and excitement are similar enough that fear can be turned to excitement for positive results. The distance from fear to calm is too large to overcome with affirmations. To be valuable, feedback should mesh with the possibilities. Calm in front of a crowd isn't a possibility for many people but the heart-thumping can be excitement rather than fear and finding the excitement can transform jitters into positive energy with the right feedback. The right feedback is provided with time to process and think rather than overwhelming with too much information. That can be rule two and a half.

The **third rule** of feedback is that it should be kind, if possible. Explaining to an ESL student that it is pronounced "guitar", without a long 'e' sound in English, or explaining to an African-American youth that it is pronounced "asked" rather than "axed" in Standard English is sensitive feedback. Language and dialects are a part of our cultural heritage. They define us. People judge based on how closely aligned our speech is with Standard English, so the feedback is important but difficult to impart without causing defensiveness. Finding the positive even if it is "nice socks" is never a waste of time if it is followed by a truthful evaluation.

The **fourth rule** of feedback is to recognize boundaries. We've all noticed stale breath or BO or piercings or tattoos or the list goes on. Certain odors are diet-based so sensitivity in olfactory feedback is respectful of differences. Unless it's a failed date who asks for the real reason you don't want to go out again there is little need to tell anyone they stink. And, if you do, rule number three still applies.

The last rule of feedback is not to fix other people's mistakes. Offer guidance but let them fix their own mistakes. The most valuable feedback I have received over my years of teaching has been self-generated. This isn't because I am a brilliant evaluator, but because when we learn lessons from our experiences we tend to listen. I am a cartwheeling cheerleader and a harsh critic of my own attempts in the classroom, sometimes within the course of minutes.

Question for Reflection:

Self-Assess for this one: Which of the rules are you best at and which do you want to improve upon to help students learn?

____

____

____

____

____

____

____

____

Real Writing Response:

My son was born two weeks early while my husband was across the country for an interview in Connecticut. I was watching Saturday Night Live with two dogs and a bowl of popcorn when my water broke so I drove my truck to the local hospital. My doctor was out of town, so the attending physician and a couple school friends were my only company. I shoo-ed them away and got massages from one sweet nurse and weathered a long night in which I was repeatedly told I may need to be air-lifted to Salt Lake City because Bozeman, Montana, did not have the equipment necessary for Preeclampsia. And I got my first A- of graduate school based on some group work I didn't get to participate in for the week I missed as a result of child delivery. My next son was born in July. I wasn't taking chances that I would earn another A-.

The A- earned that spring semester colors my judgment of Dr. Landing because it was not fair. It was my final semester in a doctoral program full of support and As. In a class the previous semester he asked if he could share my dissertation preparation paper as an example for the class. The doctoral students in my program talked of pedagogy and philosophy but didn't listen much. I was flattered to be chosen as a 'star' amongst the brilliance on display, even if my 'star' quality came from organization more than original thinking. This is the kind of positive feedback that I thrive upon, along with As.

Dr. Landing also taught a class on the history of higher education. There were two of us in the class and it lasted for three hours. We sat in an office conference room and took notes as he lectured the two of us for hours each Tuesday night. There were literally no discussions. The break was a welcome relief to escape the droning of a professor standing close enough to read my notes. I couldn't even doodle. It was structured torture.

The feedback I received from Dr. Landing has provided me with some guidance over the years. The negative feedback of receiving an unearned A- has led to my extremely tolerant and generous attitude when life-emergencies occur for my students. I understand and did not like when those were not provided for me. The A still must be earned; but time and care and support can be provided. Only then can we judge fairly and learn from our mistakes. Granted, I was an over-confident naïve student who believed she could schedule delivery for Spring Break. Oh, the lessons I have learned.

The experience of having my paper shared as an 'exemplar' was positive feedback that I try to recreate in my own classroom. I refer to students' papers and teaching and ideas and give them credit when I learn from them as often as possible. Even if Dr. Landing's approval is seen for what it is, it is appreciated and repeated just as independent projects are devised in partial response to those torturous Tuesday evening hours in his class. We learn from positive and negative experiences and feedback and more.

Learning Moment:

Critique isn't automatically negative. I don't judge the rappers I listen to or a brilliant author like George Saunders for using slang or sentences so complicated they make my head spin. Some forms of writing are allowed artistic license. Critique is positive when we use evaluations as maps for growth. The feedback teachers deliver come in many forms from grades to comments on papers to the selection of whose paper is used as an 'exemplar' for the class. Feedback based on high expectations stimulates growth and development, but fair is expected in the classroom. Even when delivered nicely, feedback is often taken defensively. The feedback we internalize as fodder for growth depends on the situation and the incentives for improvement.

Academics for Critical Literacy

Critical literacy is not easily definable. It is related to that voice in your head that reminds you that your life will not automatically become the dream on the screen if you go buy this brand of shoes or that sporty-car. It relates to the question 'why' when confused or the question 'who' when reading a text, as in 'who wrote this and why?' It is the critical eye toward finding misrepresentations or overrepresentations of certain groups of people. Like 'dead white guys' on the English lit syllabus or 'young African-American males' on the news and asking "why?" once again. Kohl (2005) recreates a 'typical' textbook entry on Rosa Parks that demonstrates why textbooks are often worthy of critical literacy. It calls "Rosa" tired and claims the Montgomery Bus Boycott happened because "other African Americans in Montgomery heard this [the news of her arrest] and they became angry too" (p.7). It dismisses race-issues as a problem of the past, portrays MLK as a savior rather than explaining that "this was a concerted effort by a determined community willing to take great risks to make democracy live" (Kohl, 2005, p. 52). Critical literacy means looking for the Truth with a capital "T", with an awareness that the truth is a matter of perspective.

Critical literacy leads me to wonder why I was never taught the story of Ho Chi Min in school. Ho Chi Minh is the only person to ever fight a war with the United States and win. So far. Individual battles with the government mounted from within, such as the 'battle' of the right to voting privileges for women or the battle to free a wrongly-convicted person, are possible exceptions. Ho Chi Minh's exact history is a bit fuzzy but it is generally believed that he spent the years from 1912-1918 in New York City. He was a worker on a French ship and got off the ship for a few years but much of that story is lost. Servicemen who fought alongside him during WWII were sometimes asked about NYC and his fondness for the city was apparent. He played a role in WWII as a rescuer of US pilots shot down by the Japanese before returning home and becoming the communist leader of his country. He based his rule on the *Declaration of Independence*, a document that he studied so much that he memorized the content. He led the struggle against French rule and threw off the oppression of the colonizers. Why was Rosa Parks part of my history but Ho Chi Minh was not?

We can study Ho Chi Minh to avoid a disaster like the Vietnam War. Maybe; I don't know the whole story. Did he turn bad? Oppress his countrymen and women? We teach students critical literacy, so they recognize the grays of the world despite a system often aligned with 'black' and 'white' mentality. We use critical literacy because the old saying 'everybody has their story' is a rare truth. We can't process all the stories without an ability to boil some down to "good gal" and "bad guy". Hitler is still evil, and Mother Theresa is still a saint, but most historical figures are not as easy to categorize. Critical literacy is a level of literacy involving judgments with due consideration of the consequences of favoring one story over another. The potential for unfairness in literacy is understood through the application of critical literacy.

Question for Reflection:

How do you teach students to use critical literacy in your classroom?

____

____

____

____

____

____

Real Writing Response:

Why? The question asked 'how', but I tend to answer by starting with the rationale. Because viewpoint is subjective. Understanding that multiple views of the same incident exist is a basic tenet of moral reasoning. Recently I used a 'learning circle' format for the first time. My first exposure to the concept was in *Touching Spirit Bear*, a fabulous young-adult novel that introduced me to circle justice as a product of rich Native-American history. Gloria Steinem's *My Life on the Road* reminded me, and I believe this format has merit. In a circle, no one leads, and this circular thinking pattern found in native writing and stories seemed worthy of exploring. We went around the circle multiple times and followed guidelines for the activity:

1. Sit in a circle.
2. The 'moderator' states these guidelines: 1. New comments may only be made by the next person in the circle; 2. Respect each other by listening; 3. Only speak when it is your turn in the circle; and 4. Be aware of not taking too much time so there is time and energy for each person's voice. 5. Any interruptions or speaking out-of-turn means the moderator will pause and reiterate the relative guideline. 6. Students may "pass" if they feel their case has been stated.
3. After the first circle another 'lap' of the circle can be used to further one's opinion depending on the time and energy of the first circle.

For the first activity, I gave each student one of three points-of-view involved in a single dog-attack incident; all three viewpoints were heard without time for questions or discussion.

"Imagine you are the judge on a trial where one woman (Candy) is suing one couple (Devon and Brandy) for damages she incurred when their dog attacked her dog in the local park. Candy has vet and doctor's bills she believes should be paid by the couple. Devon is counter-suing for emotional damages caused by the ensuing argument between himself and his wife about her handling of the situation. He wants his psychotherapy bills paid. The three 'testimonials' have been heard and you must judge who should win the case."

I then told students that all three of the people have come to them to decide their guilt or lack thereof in the incident described. Our first circle question was a 'judgment' based on the testimony provided. The first student said "Candy" was not guilty and the couple was. The ruling went unanimously for Candy. No students passed, but four stated "I would need more information" rather than passing judgment. Ten added their commentary, while the remaining ten stated, "Yeah, I agree. Next," without elaborating. Frank said that Devon was an "ass" when it was his turn to share and explained that he was not a fair judge because his small dog was killed by a Pit Bull while on leash. As the moderator, I went last. I personalized the experience as my own and admitted to being "Devon" in the incident, and let students know that parts were fictionalized. There was no actual suit or psychotherapy bills, and only a minor disagreement between my husband and myself because he stayed to help the man off the creek and I wanted to get out of the woods because the man yelling obscenities at our dogs really did freak me out. The student who called me an 'ass' blushed profusely. My point was to show students that POV matters very much and that it is okay to disagree. If I told my story from only my viewpoint (which I have done multiple times now) then the person listening generally agrees that my dog was not at fault. I am not sure I could convince Frank given his experience (the trauma of having a dog killed in front of me makes me want to cry just thinking about it), but the sentiments expressed are much different than if I came in and told the class just my own story. That is what most of us do and we are biased. Recognizing bias is a crucial part of critical literacy.

The next fill-in-the-blank activity went fine and then it was time to discuss field. The questions shared ranged from engagement issues to the logistics of a fifty-dollar art budget. The lessons learned ranged from 'over-prepare' to 'beware technology' to 'find your own voice' and 'balance' in the classroom. Conner, who I knew to be an excellent student, showed true genius. The depth to which he summed up our comments was the level needed to truly challenge a system. We cannot control the lessons of the field, but we can discuss them in a setting where critical literacy is employed. Some of us are learning what not to do and some want to know what our teachers did to get to this state-of-affairs and some of us are learning that teaching can look very different and still be excellent. The lessons we teach and learn every-day in the classroom depend on processing that is considerate and relevant to varying degrees based on our own powers of critical thinking.

Learning Moment:

Critical literacy is about justice. Kohlberg's moral reasoning is based on a sense of justice, and helps students become thinking members of a democracy without prescribing what should be believed. It is the responsibility of the education system to try to teach students how to think, rather than what to think. Critical literacy is a practical application of moral reasoning. Exposure to divergent perspectives is one way to build moral reasoning skills and critical literacy reminds us that perspective is all we have.

Academics for Goal Setting

Goals in the academic setting are statements about the long-term positive changes we plan to accomplish. We set goals that are SMART (Specific, Measurable, Attainable, Realistic and Time-Bound); in fact, one of my goals can be to write a SMART goal as an example. I believe that one is measurable and so realistic that I can do it right now.

SMART Goal #1*: Finish a draft of this section of the chapter before leaving on a college-tour over spring break.*

Is it **specific**? Yes, this section does not have a page-number limit or requirement, but it has the same four sections as other chapter sections.

It is **measurable**? There is a simple 'done' or 'not done' quality to a goal of writing a draft. The quality of that draft is not identified. For me, a draft means it is ready to be sent to a reviewer or colleague. A draft is not unedited and unrevised; it is considerate of the time of the reader. I set my own standards, so the measurement is subjective once again.

Is it **attainable**? This section has been in progress for a while, so a draft is attainable too. And realistic doesn't seem much different than attainable. Both 'qualifiers' seem to place limits on dreams. I have a textbook quote that says, "one day these phones may even be able to take pictures" when explaining the wonders of cell phones. "Ooohhh....Aaahhh"... I can imagine the students reading this with great enthusiasm as the mini-computers in their pockets buzz with memes and Instagram messages.

Is it **realistic**? No one thought it was realistic when someone first spoke of a man on the moon, so finding the balance between realistic and attainable without limiting dreams is a challenging goal. But, yes, the bar is low when only a draft is required so a draft is both attainable and realistic.

Is it **Time-Bound**? Yes. Teachers know the value of setting a deadline. Mine can be flexible. I will be reworking this after I get feedback and I understand that one section is slow progress but to be realistic we are aware of time. I am a working mother and teacher and time is always of the essence. Always! (Can you imagine the crack of a whip sounding here?)

Goals are supported by objectives, which provide stepping-stones toward progress.

So, the objectives for this chapters' draft:

- Relate goals to real writing.
- Tell a good story or two to support the importance of goal setting. *Does this one even need to be supported? I mean really, who could argue against goal setting? As a list-maker and habitual goal setter can I think of reasons not to set goals? Continual self-improvement gets tiring, so we all need brain and snack breaks but even that is not a reason to not set goals. For my brain*

break I ran a mile and that relates to separate goals of fitness and the eating of chocolate.

- Because the setting of goals is unquestionably important this section will have more questions than examples to support. So, the objective is to get you thinking about your own goals.

What are your goals? In education continual progress is the aim and setting goals is a clear step in the right direction. Naming our goals gives us a reason to get up in the morning and a path to follow. In education we are not always forward marching, but over time our record is positive. The difficulty at times is balancing our goals with the goals of others and finding shared paths toward progress, and, remembering to take a break.

Questions for Reflection:

What is your overarching goal in teaching?

____

____

____

____

What are your top five content-area goals for the classroom?

____

____

____

____

____

____

____

____

____

____

____

____

How do your classroom goals align with the goals of your school community, and general progress in the real world?

____

____

____

____

____

____

Real Writing Response:

I keep a continuous improvement goal list and multiple to-do lists so I am well acquainted with goal setting and the pressures caused by conflicting priorities. "Be a good wife and mom" are constants on the list and lately "writing time" takes precedent. I have fun items such as "learn to sail" and "paint the cottage bathroom pink" on the list too and "teach Ryan that the par-tay lifestyle is not as glamorous as it looks" has been on there for a long time. This lesson is a slow one as we guide him toward smart decisions as a teenager. My goals also include "stop whining" based on a recent discussion with my other teenage son. My goals vary but the general goal of being a positive contributing member of multiple communities can cause conflict unless priorities are clear. Thus, the importance of setting goals and remembering to keep them smart. Once our basic needs are met the goals we set tend to become intertwined with our role in the community as a moral being.

Goal #1: Be less of a perfectionist

Goal #2: Stay focused on goal #1

Goal #3: World peace and health and progress in all things that improve the human condition, one human at a time. There, that should cover it. Oops, back to #1.

I love cleanliness and order and have some perfectionist tendencies. But, this is clearly not a SMART goal. There are not specifics, and how would it be measured? Would I finally meet my goal when I let the dishes pile up or the bathroom go unpainted? The lack of a time-bind on a goal means it is one in which we strive towards continuous improvement. Which is fine if we perceive the world as one that is progressing quite nicely and one in which getting outdoors in the sunshine and eight hours of sleep and feeling productive yet relaxed is realistic and attainable. Production can be a merciless tyrant driving us forward for goals that are society-based and not always healthy. Perfectionism is not a healthy pursuit and yet the pursuit of excellence is encouraged in our society and the mixed messages are confusing. Setting goals that align with our personal missions makes sense. If our mission is to teach critical thinking and real-world skills, then the classroom is a place to thrive and make a difference. If our goal is to find balance and move forward, then our outcomes can be achieved. If the goal is perfection, then it is unrealistic and unattainable.

Learning Moment:

The lesson is that we constantly set goals and either achieve or fail. If we make progress some days that is enough and sometimes we set the bar too low and other days we set it too high and we constantly adjust and move forward. Life is not a race, and goals that coalesce with our sense of purpose in the classroom must be SMART and aligned with the goals of the larger community to provide data that matters. Like smiles, but that is too low of a bar. Critical thinking and moral reasoning are high bars and raising the bar is our only constant in education. Jump, teachers and students, jump seems to be the goal in assessment.

Chapter Four: Diversity Matters

If literacy is the swing in education, diversity is the rocket. Equality. Acceptance. Fairness. Justice. These concepts are foundational for a positive schooling experience no matter the make-up of the student body. Diversity is related to all the earlier chapters. Who you are and the foundations of literacy overlap. The link between assessment and diversity is evident because schools demand a level of conformity. We prepare with standards and measure with standardized tests. Normed and referenced curriculum is an equalizer of expectations, but the cost to creativity and acceptance of differences is considered here as we move forward. This chapter moves our focus beyond the test and back to students, where it belongs.

The topic of diversity in education has expanded since the Civil Rights movement to such an extent that it is a major emphasis across content areas. The research on the achievement gap and models for how to erase that gap continue. Stories of segregation and IQ-tests being used to place second-language speakers in classrooms for 'retarded' students are a part of our history and we continue to root out and correct errors. The improvements made in how children, women, minorities, and the poor are treated are substantial and ongoing in our education system. That deserves celebration and continued vigilance.

We learn the culture of family in our formative years and the culture of school either reinforces or it causes us to question our earlier learning; most education provides a confusing mix of both. We learn about cultures and diversity through experiences. My family traveled extensively. Trips to visit family in San Francisco and to DC to see the monuments were punctuated by dude ranches in Colorado and Wyoming and backcountry camping with horses in the Bighorns. We traveled with large groups of elderly partiers from the Midwest when I was in my teens. We showed up in front of the LA Biltmore—a beautiful building with luxurious rooms and cultured sommeliers in every restaurant—,with luggage on top of the van. Wearing cowboy hats and bolo ties. I felt like that lame-ol' song by Donny and Marie.

I'm a little bit country.

And I'm a little bit rock n' roll.

These corny child singers were part of a happy childhood. Despite a troubling teenage and young-adult phase, I survived and thrived as a new teacher. That is the best phrase ever when you want to discuss drugs, dancing, pool halls, pain, confusion, joy and a series of boyfriends without details. I was still learning about diversity and unreflective of my privilege. Even as a broke college-student and waitress who lived with drag queens and cockroaches I always had money enough and food enough and love and support and warmth enough and health enough to consider myself blessed. Privileged. Which directly relates to the topic of diversity with much White guilt and questions of 'just deserts' for me. Acknowledging that my leg-up impacted my choices is part of understanding diversity and Whiteness. If we see the students for who they are and try to guide them toward learning without judging harshly based on circumstances beyond a child's control, then Whiteness will no longer be a screen that clouds our judgment. Or, it will at least be an acknowledged part of the terministic screen.

Resiliency can be earned through hardship, but one does not need to overcome great odds to be resilient. Agency is gained through self-awareness and appreciation for the causes and effects of our lifestyle. The lessons we teach that lead students to understand and accept differences and treat others with respect and compassion all involve diversity, no matter who is in the room. Since reading McIntosh (1996) I have understood that my privilege means I didn't work as hard for my agency. What I do with that agency is the true test for me. I choose to explore diversity and believe it is my responsibility to speak about it because this is a way to contribute. Whether you consider mine a legitimate voice in the discussion of diversity or just another White woman talking more than she listens is up to you.

This chapter includes:

- The complication of cultural capital,
- The legitimacy power struggle,
- The language of your classroom, and,
- Race, class, and gender—hot button topics in relation to Real Writing.

It is commonly known that standardized tests measure your cultural capital more than aptitude (Abeles, 2015). So, after a consideration of the fact that we all judge, now we get into our most challenging subject for many classrooms. It's been here all along and it contains some violence beyond the wig-beating mentioned earlier. Buckle in and expect some awkward pauses, folks; we are diving into diversity. Providing an equal education for those whose English is not standard to start and those who lack cultural capital due to factors of race, class or gender rather than abilities is a necessity for progress. This is how we legitimize the rules in our culture.

Discussion Questions for Real Writing Practice:

- How do you prepare for critical conversations relating to culture?
- What can you do to advocate for equity at your school?
- What do you believe the results would be if you surveyed your school about hot-button topics?
- What language differences are evident in your classroom?

Academics for Cultural Capital

A lack of awareness of cultural capital can lead teachers to misinterpret students' actions as deviant, and treat them punitively or lower expectations (Delpit, 1997/2002). "Take off your baseball cap and stay in your seat." So much control—what you wear and where you go—held by schools is wielded without considering the communication styles and resistance of the students striving towards independence. At-risk students are the ones who possess the least cultural capital and are most likely to be resistant to traditional education.

According to Baldwin (1955) this is a positive because any black man who takes education at face-value is going to get disillusioned. Minorities are the ones most likely to be given directives, to be disadvantaged by tracking, and to be negatively impacted by schooling if considerations are not made. This is unfair regardless of time-period and still happening today. Education can disappoint.

Most people don't like to be told what to do. How to think. What to think. How to act. Yet, if you don't possess cultural capital you are more likely to be treated with directives. This is the opposite of the knapsack; it is the yoke of oppression. Based on the way we interact, students can view schools as supportive allies or jailers. Based on how we interact, respect is either given or taken or shared. Peggy McIntosh (2003) was my introduction to cultural capital and whiteness. The invisible backpack of privilegc is unpacked with an awareness that the level of reflection requires wisdom and moral reasoning that needs to be slowly developed.

Question for Reflection:

What do you bring with you in your 'backpack' of privilege each day?

____

____

____

____

____

____

Real Writing Response:

I feel confident that I can demand respect in most social situations. That is my cultural capital. If someone tells me I can kiss their ass, chances are my impression will be negative. So, a misunderstanding can be critical in communication issues. If someone says, "eat your mother" and giggles it is nice to have a native-speaker in the car. Preferably Mexican and educated and able to communicate clearly also. It was not luck that the man in the car was our Spanish teacher. He ran our classes and knew this was the fastest way to understand Mexico. To experience it with a safe translator and guide. After that I ventured forth on my own. I knew all the swear words, what more could I need? Money, experience and an invincible spirit are all in my backpack.

Some of my most important backpack items include a sense of agency, a belief that I am a good person, an excellent learner, and a fair judge of character. And, if I get lost I am likely to receive help because most strangers are not afraid of a well-groomed White woman. I didn't need to know how to read a map in New York City. People walked up to my sister-in-law and myself and offered to help us find our way. That is all in my backpack. The ability to look slightly befuddled in such a way that complete strangers offer a ride and their trust is in there too. And the ability to fit in where I don't quite belong. Instead of being a heavy load, my backpack is like the vanishing bag in Harry Potter. It carries more than seems possible and the weight remains feather light.

My family moved to a small touristy-farming community fourteen years ago based on data and more. We looked at average incomes and scores for schools and considered many different communities but decided one was 'too high-pressured' when the real-estate agent told us about the competitive preschool for success. Another was deemed 'too redneck' after a trip to the local ice-cream shop revealed a serious dental issue and the local beach was an appalling sludge. Still another was ruled out because there was no actual town, only strip malls and parking lots. The numbers helped us select a place to live, but the numbers could never sum up the intricacy of living in a community like Frankenmuth.

Our neighbor Less said, "The best day of your life is the day you die," practically as we shake hands for introductions. I reserve judgment, but I struggle with that opener and find the regular claiming of faith upon introduction to be off-putting. "What church do you attend?" seemed an intrusive question that was repeated for months. Our move to a small isolated community landed my family in the "bubble". Figuring out who is here because of a fear of the outside and who is here for the terrific community takes time and nuanced discussions that no numbers could replace. Conversations and connections are important too and those are enhanced when we share similar cultural capital. We know how to communicate with each other respectfully.

I do not possess much cultural capital in Frankenmuth. I do not bear a distinguished German name and am an oddity as a Smith. I am not Lutheran, and my family is *gasp* liberal; even those who do not know me judge my status of professor and assume the worst. I am an 'other' here in ways I have rarely felt and yet I chose to raise my children here. Sometimes the religious references are comical, such as when a neighbor boy misquotes Jesus in his defense for hitting back. "Jesus says we should strike the other's cheek." I was less amused when he asked my sons' friends, "Are you Christian? I'm not allowed to play with anyone who's not." I was even less amused when white crosses started appearing in all the neighborhood yards. For that we turned back to numbers, as in "twelve out of fifteen houses on this block have a cross in their yard;" and, "how do you think the two Indian families in town feel about this or singing Christmas Carols in music class." And, are there any actual Jewish families in Frankenmuth?

In Arizona there is a route between Phoenix and Las Vegas where white crosses are present around every corner. It is a winding two-lane highway apparently known for its fatalities. Each cross marks the spot where someone died in an accident. Some of the crosses are surrounded by flowers or mementos, a shrine of sorts to the beloved family member who never made it home. So, when I first noticed the white crosses in the flowerbeds around Frankenmuth I wondered if a similar shrine was the intent. Is that the spot where Grandma Gretel or Uncle Aldo keeled over in the shade of an elm? Was she tending the petunias and her heart gave out? Was he blowing the leaves out of the yard and got attacked by a squirrel?

The crosses started years ago when an outsider talked of suing the city to remove the cross from the Frankenmuth flag. Frankmuthians showed their support of the cross by putting simple white crosses in yards and argued that their history as a missionary outpost justified the cross on the flag. If the cross is a sign that someone with Christian ideals lives in that home, then "go to any house with a cross for help" would be good advice to my children. Or "surround yourself with Christly-people" but that can turn into a 'stick-to-your-own' mentality that isn't felt or believed in my family. For others the crosses could be a 'keep out if you're not Christian' symbol.

Yet, I love Frankenmuth, despite my lack of a cross and my aversion to church-and-state integration. I cannot quantify the belief that this community is one big family where we all care about each other's children and families to varying extents. Our lack of cultural capital in town does not diminish the supportive and caring atmosphere in the schools and community. This belief is what makes Frankenmuth a positive choice for my family despite the crosses in the yards and the proselytizing. Instead I feel honored to be invited and thankful that we are welcome despite the Buddha statue in my flowerbed instead. This gentle cocoon of religious tolerance for those with a cross in their yard is a wonderful home.

Learning Moment:

What I bring in my backpack to Frankenmuth and many community settings is a cultural capital that allows me to feel 'at home' in divergent situations because I feel the powers-that-be are backing me. That feeling of 'owning it' is an amazing benefit I see as my 'just deserts' until I am reflective and remember that I started out with more advantages than most. White guilt is not a negative, just an awareness of unfairness and a vow to fix the messes of our ancestors so that everyone can 'own it'. If we stop fighting for pieces of the pie we can figure out how to increase the recipe, so no one goes hungry for basic rights. Even if we aren't directly responsible, many of us have directly benefited and being part of the solution is the best atonement for the inequities of the magic backpack of privilege. Unpacking is a personal voyage for each of us and I choose generally not to unpack in front of strangers unless it is in writing. Writing is the right tool for unpacking metaphorically because we can explore ideas and decide which response is best for the situation.

Academics for Legitimacy

Respect is a term bandied about regularly in relation to diversity. Aretha sings about it and teachers talk about it but a common definition and research support do not exist. In contrast, legitimacy is a researched (Gladwell, 2015) concept that includes three components:

1. A voice for those without power

An example: Starbuck's provided this to two black men arrested in a Philadelphia branch of the franchise. They acknowledged the incident and apologized to the nation by closing their stores on May 29th. I choose to interpret this symbolic gesture as a true recognition that policies need to change. Thus, I see Starbucks as an institution trying to provide a 'voice' to those ruled by society's policies and laws.

2. Predictability—rules will be similar day-to-day

This is where Starbuck's generally shines. We all get charged the same amount for the same products and the consistency in prices and offerings and policies is well recorded.

3. Fairness—different groups are treated justly

At my local Starbucks I often encounter diversity and notice that the staff treats us all the same. I hope that I treat people equally as well. I have not encountered any overt lack of respect for groups or individuals.

***The legitimization of Starbucks is mine; Gladwell uses more intellectual topics for his examples.

Gladwell explains the principles of legitimacy in relation to law and order and the unrest in Northern Ireland that resulted in The Troubles, a thirty-year conflict between Protestants and Catholics. The brutality of this guerrilla war could have been avoided if the British forces established legitimacy rather than forcing curfews and unfair laws upon the Catholics. They were beaten, riots erupted, and children were starving because they were not allowed out of their homes. The police launched teargas at

Catholic women pushing prams full of milk and supplies to feed children. This persecution strengthened Catholic resolve. Eventually, saner heads prevailed, the deliveries were allowed, and a tentative peace was established. The British ruling forces were outsiders imposing their control on the Irish Catholics. Rather like a teacher who does not share an understanding of legitimacy.

What I realize after years of observing students practicing their teaching, is that my students often lack legitimacy because it is developed with time and experience. I observed a classroom where the intern had them popcorn-reading a story aloud while students summersaulted through the room. Few students were engaged with listening and following along. I observed an intern clap in a pattern for "attention" and the students in the room ignored her and just talked louder. She kept on clapping. Some classroom leaders are unaware of the natural pace of a classroom and others just aren't 'with-it' enough. They are not legitimate teachers, yet. While many would say these teachers need to learn how to improve 'discipline', Gladwell proposes that what they need is legitimacy. The best way to get that is through experience.

As teachers, we often question our own legitimacy. What do I, a Starbuck's-loving, privileged White woman have that makes me a legitimate voice of diversity? What do you, fill-in-your-own-blanks, know about being a legitimate voice for diversity? We don't have to share a common culture to establish respect. We just need to be legit.

Question for Reflection:

How can you be legit if you don't share a culture with your students?

____

____

____

____

____

____

____

Real Writing:

What does the word 'legitimacy' conjure up in your mind? Does the old song "2 legit 2 quit" by M.C. Hammer start playing and maybe some connection to the word 'bastard' sally forth? Many of the stories that I recount about my urban teaching experiences involve violence. How do I tell the story of the riot without adding to the perception of others as 'violent' and inner-cities as dangerous places? How do I tell of Pilar's twelve people living in a one-bedroom apartment and not reinforce stereotypes of Hispanics?

Stories of difference are the ones that fascinate us and telling our real story builds legitimacy, but it can often lead to fear rather than comprehension. I remember one fight from my high school experience as a student. In the darkened hallway two boys were quickly circled by other students. A few punches were thrown before a teacher intervened and we all shuffled off without incident while the boxers were escorted to the office. It shares the same tepid level of excitement as the pep assemblies held there, rather like watching the grass grow. Then I went to Flint Northern and the dance team writhed and the energy of the crowd; it was electric. I was out of my realm and knew it. Most of us feel out of our realm regarding diversity but a deeper awareness is only possible with reflection.

My first fight at Flint Northern started with me rushing out of my classroom because all the students surged out during the passing period. Voices were raised. A disturbance. One girl was sitting on the back of another girl who was prone in the hallway. Blood was on the floor and the girl on top was pulling hair and scratching at eyes and appeared ready to slam her victim's head on the tiles, so I instinctively stepped in and tried to pull the top girl off before more blood could be spilled. Luckily, a security guard was close at hand and the back-up quickly relieved me of the handful of squirming, kicking, clawing rage that I didn't have a clue how to control. I was told in no uncertain terms to "never, ever" step into the middle of a fight again. Stories of the crowd turning ugly and teachers getting punched were lessons shared from first-hand perspectives.

The next time there was pandemonium in the halls was also during a passing period. This time the students ran into my room rather than out and many were unfamiliar. "Gun" was repeated and we took cover behind desks and overturned chairs. Security came through and the day continued within minutes with no official coverage ever shared. I didn't even get a memo for communication. Violence just was. The story of a boy being kicked on the ground drawing a gun and shooting into the ceiling was the explanation shared in the teacher's lounge. I was relieved no one got shot and that my catfight experience happened so that I knew not to run toward the trouble.

I didn't run toward the next violence I encountered but I did walk through it with a dumbfounded look on my face. The riot squad in Phoenix, dressed all in black with billy-clubs, five-foot shields and gas masks firmly in place piled out of buses and vans like a scene from a war zone. There were at least fifty officers in full gear and throwing tear gas within minutes of a small riot erupting on campus. On my way from the lunch room I saw a teen pull a six-foot stake holding a tree up out of the ground and swing it around his head, threatening rivals. I hustled into my classroom and was on 'lock-down' but left the room regularly to wander the hallway and get updates on the situation. I recall talking to teachers I'd never spoken with before that day and a sense of camaraderie amongst those of us contained together. There was a student-teacher being observed who had to continue her lesson as though unaffected by the circling of six helicopters and the arrival of the National Guard. My class was watching the incident on the television (the helicopters were mostly news) and I had an aide in the classroom. Plus, the students wanted my updates, so I felt justified in venturing forth as long as I didn't get in the way of the SWAT team. I'd learned not to run toward the trouble, but I still wanted to see the action.

The next action that stands out vividly was a drive-by shooting. It was the end of the school day at South Mountain High School and I was driving my Tracker toward the entrance. I had the soft-top up and the tunes jamming and was probably planning my evening meeting of friends when a large tank-of-a-car pulled across the entry of the school and someone rolled out of the backseat and started firing toward the crowd. Next to me. I ducked, as did the kids walking down the sidewalk. Choreographed moves couldn't have been more in sync. Stop, drop, and roll. I climbed out from under the dash and peered over the steering wheel as the shooter got back in the boat-of-a-car and kept driving. No one cried or made a scene. I drove out of the lot and to my own neighborhood where the police would arrive if a drunken student got too loud, let alone a shooting. After the riot, this small incident of violence never even registered on the news.

At South Mountain I pretended my 'gang' students were just part of a club for recent immigrants and their "Wet Back Power—WBP" tattoos and hand-signs were not indicative of any of the crimes associated with street gangs. My students were young men and women who took care of themselves for the most part. 'Mine' were good kids. I loved most, in a maternal teacher-y kind of way. Violent stories stand out because of the stress and novelty and my sharing of them is to advocate for change. I find it reprehensible that everyone went about their day as though nothing out of the ordinary happened after most of these occurrences. There was no news coverage of the shooting. I was one of one-hundred witnesses, literally, and none of us chose to report it. Trying to be legitimate with these students meant caring about them and learning to live with violence in the background. The stress of teaching without support in an inner-city school is nothing compared to the stress of living in a neighborhood of violence. Teaching is partially about using legitimate means to eradicate violence in our schools, and real writing is one tool in our belt, so to speak.

Learning Moment:

Legitimacy is based on three tenets that allow teachers to establish an atmosphere of respect and it is extremely individualized. I could not have Mrs. Timm's brand of classroom management because I never lived where

I teach. If we work to be fair, to give students voice, and to build a climate that prioritizes predictability over surprise then we legitimize our classrooms. If we develop engaging lessons and change activities to keep staleness at bay and give students voice by listening to them and learning along with them then we take strides in building respect. Throw in a little discipline and you can teach anywhere if you possess the content knowledge and the desire to make a positive difference. You can never be too legit to quit learning.

Academics for Language in the Classroom

As soon as someone opens his or her mouth and speaks the listeners start making assumptions about gender, race, class, age, and level of education in addition to other pieces of background information. Those who speak with Southern accents are assumed less intelligent and those who speak with British accents are assumed more intelligent and our interactions are impacted. We favor Standard English in schools and other languages, dialects, and even accents are treated as 'less' or 'more' depending on their association with the language of power. Lisa Delpit's vignette at the start of *The Skin that We Speak* (2002) demonstrates the importance of speech with a study that involved playing two voice-recordings to kindergarten students and then asking a series of questions. Stereotyping based on the dialect indicate that the speaker who used Ebonics was considered 'in need', although all the kids indicated that they'd rather play with their own kind. We are all most comfortable around those whose language is similar to our own.

Beyond the bias of dialects and second languages, the way we speak matters. Volume, accent, word-choice and the tendency to phrase statements as questions even when we are giving directions can all lead to communication problems. Delpit (2002/2005) explains the quagmire of language nuances and the communication breakdown that occurs when those in power assume that children of different backgrounds share communication patterns when, in fact, those patterns vary. Her positions are supported by seminal works such as Heath (1983) and once again, common sense. Language differences are often the cause of failure in our schools and this discrimination limits students' chances of success. We didn't need the research to know this, but the supporting evidence is clear.

The basic research on linguistics shows that:

1. There are no "primitive" languages: all languages are equally complex and equally capable of expressing any idea in the universe. Just because the Eskimos have multiple words for snow doesn't mean others can't get the listener or reader to understand the concept. Not quite like the Eskimo, but that seems fair since they are stuck living in it year-round.

2. All grammars contain rules for the formation of words and sentences of a similar kind. The double-negative in Ebonics, for example, follows a distinctive set of rules that can be traced back to an African language commonly used by early slaves.

3. Every language has a way of referring to past time, negating, forming questions, issuing commands, and so on. The nuances of these ways can cause misunderstandings. I ask my students to get out paper and pencil to write. Do you 'tell' yours or ask? It matters in the classroom when the language of power fails to recognize and account for these differences in ways that support all learners.

4. The differences we find among languages cannot be due to biological reasons.

Question for Reflection:

What is the significance of your language in the classroom? What kind of language do you hear?

____

____

____

____

____

____

____

____

Real Writing Response:

Anyone who does not believe language is important has most likely not experienced being in a situation where her language skills are deficient. It lends an interesting degree of poignancy to the situation that is impossible to get in a classroom unless language is directly addressed.

You might say I am learned in languages. Or you may not because that sounds pretentious, so you'd say I learned my lessons. Either way, your word choice tells enough about you that these lessons once again start before schooling and continue each year as new words like 'mansplaining' enter the lexicon. I don't keep up with slang beyond staying two steps behind my own teens, but languages never fail to fascinate me. Which was why I taught a lesson on Ebonics to a classroom of all African-American students at Flint Northern High school, as a student-teacher. When I announced I would be teaching 'Black English' the students were skeptical.

"What dis white girl gonna teach us about Black English?" was not an unreasonable question. "Black? Who you calling Black? My skin is mahogany," also seemed a reasonable distinction. The grumblings increased, and I considered my next move. I thank the spitfire who told class, "Y'all shut up, I want to hear what she's got-ta say." I stood in front of the white projector screen and made a joke about not really being White either when you look at the color of the screen. "More of a pinkish off-white spotted brown" was how I described my freckled skin at twenty-two in front of my first heckling audience.

Then I shared my fascination and the rules that Black English follows and traced the African history. I shared speech patterns and then did a lesson on slang. I let them know I thought it was unfair to make them learn Standard English but that I wanted them to have the opportunities it provides. If I was teaching the lesson today I would also joke about how my husband says "bubbler" instead of water-fountain or about how he overcompensates for his 'r-less-ness' by saying 'idear'. At the time my personal connection was about how my mother always corrected me when I said, "me and Karen" by saying "Karen and I" and then I'd respond "no, you aren't coming with us" and laugh. Mom always got my sense of humor and didn't seem to take it personally. I read her body language too.

Driving down to the coast in Mexico with Fiona Margot and two other teachers was a common occurrence during my three years teaching in

Maricopa. On this trip we were cruising a deserted highway when flashing lights behind us indicated to pull over. What flashes through your head with those lights? What went through mine was “oh god, please don’t take us to a Mexican prison or worse with your gun and authority in a foreign country known for mysterious disappearances and corruption”. What showed on my face was a smile and compliance. It said, “Just take my money and leave in peace, please.”

Fiona was confident and talkative and probably nervous despite the playful banter. The officer was smiling when he complimented her Spanish and then she responded, and his look changed. The man with us was from Mexico and quickly took over, speaking fast and explaining. Some would call this mansplaining, but that definition would be wrong. He did not condescend. He paid the police officer a little extra bribe money and we waved, and the officer drove off and we all sagged with relief. What did Fiona say? When the officer complimented her Spanish she thought she said, “ha-ha, right, like your mother” in a playful way. As in, I speak just like your mom. What she said was “ha-ha, right, eat your mother.” Rather insulting.

Taking it personally is more the norm than the exception with language. The officer didn’t take it personally but the fine increased. How we talk reflects who we are and if corrected in a way that does not acknowledge the speaker’s value then bad vibes are likely. I do not correct people’s grammar or word choice unless they are students or immediate family. I have a friend who says “seen” rather than “saw”, as in “I seen your son at the store yesterday” and each time I hear it I cringe and stop myself from giving a free lesson in grammar. This same friend regularly espouses the view “if you don’t speak English, go back to your own country” and I argue with her on issues of immigration and language equality in the United States each time she espouses her view in my presence. That lesson is a moral obligation, just like telling my father-in-law not to swear in front of my young children was a moral obligation at the time.

Learning Moment:

What is 'right' and what is 'wrong' in language depends on the context and requires code-switching, alternating language to fit circumstances. Those who don't understand struggle more and the goal of schooling is to lessen learning struggles so those are addressed in the classroom and through outside support systems. What we say should be more important than how we say it, but until that is the case it is important to teach students to code switch and read each situation to determine the appropriate language to best express content.

Academics for Race, Class, and Gender

We learn our roles from early ages and the lessons of culture, class and gender are so intertwined with our being that when asked about ethnicity many in the US claim, "American as apple pie" for our background. Not that we ask, generally; it is considered rude to ask for personal information directly. In my culture, children learn 'stranger danger' and play little league ball and we learn that financial talk is vulgar and not to accept charity. We learn this and more before we understand that our lessons vary based on who our people are. While some learn that the squeaky wheel gets attention, others learn that if you don't speak up people take advantage. People of all ilk. Who are your people? The lessons we learn are the basis for our terministic screen and they impact our relationship with education in ways that are so pervasive as to be like water to the fish, often unidentified but always present.

Race

Kozol (1991) details the savage inequalities of the urban poor and yet race is a meaningless social construct with no significance beyond cultural implications. Culture, paradoxically, is all important. Red, black, brown, yellow, and white are much less important than who your parents happen to be. We each have sub-sets of culture and act, talk, and even think in diverse ways depending on the person with whom we interact. We all code switch and even change with time and circumstances, regardless of cultural origins but those origins influence our lives whether we lead an examined or an unexamined life.

Class

Money, fame, and success don't buy happiness as evidenced recently by Kate Spade and Anthony Bordaine. Yet, the advantages of wealth are evident since the beginning of time. Comforts and health are increased when your class rises but community can't be bought or it feels sterile. Jean Anyon (1981) studied how as class rises so does the freedom of the students in the classroom. If visitors walk through metal detectors and security escorts us to classrooms, then a school feels prison-esque. A community can still form and be positive, but it is challenging in poor settings, with limited funds.

Gender

Sadker and Sadker (1994) study gender fairness in the classroom. Their research shows we call on girls less often, provide them less feedback, and then don't understand why fewer thrive in finding their voice professionally. In the past this was the result of motherhood and fatherhood looking very different, now it is the result of sexism. Teachers don't need to be feminists to see the value in fairness. If treated equally then more female doctors can provide compassionate care and the best musicians can provide us with music. And, why not listen to the very best music?

Gladwell (2015) explains how gender discrimination prevalent in orchestras is being eradicated. The three most common words when considering the make-up of orchestras: old, white, and guys. Do you know what finally worked so that orchestras would no longer be 95% male musicians? Screens. When we don't 'see' the people we are judging we don't let our other impressions decide whose music sounds the best, not accounting for the quality of the instrument which brings class back into the equation even through a screen. A screen can't level the playing field, but it can improve women's chances of making it to the philharmonic. From minor annoyances to wage-differentials, gender differences are insidious and long-standing and, according to Junger (2016) unlikely to ever dissipate just like 'conservative' and 'liberal' will never go away. What can go away is the belief that one deserves 'less' because one is female; that part can change.

Reflection Question for Race, Class and Gender:

What is the best way to approach these hot-button topics in the content classroom?

____

____

____

____

____

____

____

Real Writing Response:

Writing about diversity is a top option because it gives students a chance to listen to their own thoughts and check for flaws in logic and reflect on positions. Given a racist, classist or sexist statement on paper most of us can pick it apart and refute it within minutes. If said aloud in class, there are more complications. Students are often defensive if errors in thinking are pointed out publicly. Asking students to write down their thoughts when a conversation topic in the classroom turns heated takes the student into learning mode and allows tempers to cool and saner opinions to be stated. Requiring that they consider or write out the opposing viewpoints introduces critical-thinking to the discussion. Of course, only so much writing about diversity or talking about it is necessary in many situations. There are those who are actual victims of our system and the work of empowering the voiceless is never-ending and a valuable use of time, as it applies to your content-area and context. Repeat after me, as it applies to *your* content-area and context.

Of course, our lessons in diversity don't begin when we start teaching. In the summer of 1986 Karen Schultz and I went to Chicago to visit two separate friends. Karen was my roommate and Edward was a friend of hers who recently moved to Chicago and landed a role in a play. We met at the show and then went to the after-party with Edward. This was a strange jump into the world of aspiring stars of the stage and my impressions were not positive. The people seemed full of pretensions and their snootiness was not warranted, given the quality of the production or the number of bodies sharing one small flat. This was not the Ritz. After the after-party (ah, the energy of youth) Karen and I decided to go visit Mikey, a mutual friend and past co-worker who was freshly ensconced in a luxury apartment with his new boyfriend. Cary was the most effeminate man I have met and within minutes of meeting I was referring to him as 'her' and 'she' and accompanying Cary to the lady's room at the club. I had a roommate who was a drag-queen, but this was different. This night in Chicago taught me lessons I remember years later. I learned that men can be women and the rich are often less arrogant than those with aspirations to fame. Cary was the heir-apparent to Greyhound which sold for 2.8 billion in 2007 and I still remember her kind and gentle spirit. Lessons of diversity take place in our homes and lives daily. Not only do they start at birth, they never end. Which is why writing this section feels as though it could turn into a memoir beyond the scope of this text.

We filter experiences to find supporting or conflicting evidence when a statement is made and confirm or deny based on our version of 'truth'. There are reminders everywhere that our backgrounds vary; the worker at the airport who just dished up my food did not know the word 'cauliflower' and asked, "do you want more of this white stuff?" When I said, “no, thanks, I prefer squash more than cauliflower” he repeated the word and asked about pronunciation. I can surmise that fresh veggies were not available often in his home. The complexity of this is that we look for the patterns and our ‘confirmations’ can include noticing that the Jewish shopkeeper haggles or the Asian woman is a poor driver or any number of stereotypes. We do this because we tend to notice patterns and outliers. The exception and the rule both matter in terms of diversity. The young African-American who did not recognize cauliflower serves to confirm my belief that those who grow up poor have fewer healthy food options. This is confirmed by research but anyone who considers grocery store fare in many locales knows the truth of it. We learn through experience.

Issues of race, class, and gender are as individualized as taste in food. In China I claimed to be vegetarian rather than explain, ‘if you honor me with a fish-head I may throw up a little in my mouth’. I was not adventurous enough to drink tap-water; Coca-Cola and tea, cold and hot please. I ate what may have been a pigeon and was treated like a rock star. People pointed and asked if they could get their picture taken with me. I sat and ate pizza on a stool in a little cafe, window front, and a small crowd gathered to watch me. I felt somewhat like a petting-zoo ostrich, only the brave approached. That was a diverse experience. I can top it, and you probably can too but be sure to keep it classroom appropriate and have a reason beyond a good story to tell.

Another food related diversity experience for me was being mugged leaving a Taco Bell in Flint. I had a wonderful concoction of cheese and crunchiness in my hands and a purse wrapped around my arm and when the young man ran past and grabbed my purse, I panicked. I reached for my butterfly-knife. I was just pulling it free from the purse when the mugger fell and took my purse with him and the knife skittered across the parking lot. A bystander ran over and asked, “Hey, he take yo’ bag?” and at my nod he ran after the mugger and returned shortly with my purse. Minus the cash, but still. Not terrible. No one was hurt, and I called my mom and cried rather drastically into the phone rather than reporting it to the police. I knew the cash was missing because I tried to give a reward to the young African-American man who ran after the mugger and returned my purse.

Learning Moment:

Culture, race, and gender is so prevalent once we pay attention that this section could tangent into an autobiography. I am not a tangent queen in the classroom, and that is the balance that needs found. My third-grade teacher asked me to write a scar story. We were given a blank piece of paper and told to put an ‘x’ each place we have a scar. Can you imagine this prompt as an adult? The lessons of culture, class, and gender are prevalent and influence our actions and reactions to most social situations. They never end, but this chapter must. I hope the number of lessons doesn’t overwhelm.

Chapter 5: Why design your own lessons?

Autonomy is necessary for job satisfaction, but exactly how much control do we mean? Those who teach do not generally earn 'academic freedom' until the university level. Some say "once I shut my classroom door" as though they aren't still bound by the rules, but we all know that's not accurate. I was given my first classroom with no more direction than cupboards filled with class-sets of books and no standards or curriculum shared and told "teach reading" and I did. To the best of my limited abilities and with the help of other teachers who cared about the students and each other. Nowadays, imposed standards are considered each time we design a lesson and not only is there a prescribed curriculum, there are hidden agendas and the absence of what we don't teach too. A balance can be found in this area so that autonomy doesn't result in lacking structure and focus. To find this balance, teachers need time to prepare for themselves with subject-matter and students given top consideration. Then strategies for learning are part of the pedagogy expertise required to be a teacher. To plan effective lessons, teachers link content and strategy. The value is in the connection between the two.

According to Gladwell (2008), the three components work must have to be meaningful or fulfilling are:

1. Autonomy
2. Complexity
3. A connection between effort and reward

Experts in pedagogy and content design lessons and adapt them to lead students toward their own autonomy, critical-thinking, and continued learning. If we let others design our lessons the result is that we cease to make decisions that meet learner's needs. If teachers are devalued, we move away from schools that create leaders and thinkers and toward schools that lead to repeated mistakes because we discount the role. This doesn't mean we need to reinvent the wheel each time we set off on the road to teaching a lesson, nor does it mean that teachers have free reign. It means that the complex task of teaching our children deserves to be valued and the teachers we trust to do this work must be able to make decisions about how to present the materials and convey the lessons. This is the basis for the three tenets of this chapter or components classroom work must have to be meaningful. These are in addition to Gladwell's autonomy, complexity, and recompense:

Content: This gets to be king because teachers from each angle see the importance of communication skills in connection to their subject. An artist must be able to talk to people to sell her work. A musician must be able to express the words in writing or song at some point for it to be music. There is a complicated history, but the two are forever linked since the first caveman drew a picture on the wall to boast or let his wife know where he was. (Out hunting beasts, be home before sunset, love, Ogg…) Literacy and the link to most contents is not a hard sell because it is required for all aspects of schooling from the direction on how to use the jig-saw, so no fingers are lost, to the football team memorizing plays.

Pedagogy: The strategies and methods used to convey content. See Marzano in the lesson plan format (*appendix #2*). If you can't mix and match the basics, then there is a problem. The problem can be housed in the content, the pedagogy or the context.

Context: The environment created by considering all the elements in chapters one through four. We've covered the teacher, students, literacy, assessment and diversity and now we narrow in on pedagogy. Of course, like the lessons you teach, there is overlap. The constantly lapping waves on the shores of progress require some. Some days they come together with a crash and other days the waters are calm.

In this chapter we explore the topic of selecting strategies that enhance content learning in the classroom. Beyond the high-yield methods of Marzano (appendix #2) there are the following areas to consider when creating your lessons:

- Vocabulary as the focus
- Cooperative learning
- Graphic Organizers

The proficient reader research strategies can be mixed into more configurations than could possibly be included in one text. These are like meat, cheese, and tortillas at Taco Bell. If you rely on good basics, then you can decide how best to mix the components for lessons. Beans, guacamole, hot-sauce and more can be added on top, but the more that is added the more complicated the lesson becomes. Combining elements of proficient reader research with other 'proven winners' like cooperative learning and graphic organizers is a step toward content-literacy that can improve learning. This text can't answer "what is the absolute, very best strategy?" because it depends on too many factors that are connected to the situation. This chapter delves into strategies and ways to teach with the understanding that a teacher adapts for his or her own situation.

Strategies have been a favorite of mine since graduate school. I would learn one in class and then implement it right away. Some were huge successes, like anticipation guides, and others were less of a hit, like SQ3R, based on the learning of students and the ease of implementation. I am unwilling to invest large amounts of time to strategies that complicate the process unless the payoff is high in terms of content progress. Not that I understood this when I started teaching. My first year I used a party-game book to design activities. I wrote vocabulary words on little slips of paper and put them in balloons of two different colors. Students each tied a balloon to their ankle and the game began. My lesson plan notes included gems, such as “make the string longer so no one’s ankle gets hurt”. Deep, really deep.

Sometimes we start with content. Sometimes with strategy. Sometimes with standards or goals for student learning. Sometimes with the thought that a change is needed to spice up the lesson. A cool strategy is useless unless it is linked with the content students are learning, sort of like eating a bowl of sour-cream on the side with none of the other fixin’s. The best content is useless if the students don’t interact in a way that produces learning. This is a hard part of teaching, but it is also what makes our roles as teachers exciting and autonomous. We get to add the tang of jalapeños if the students can handle it.

Discussion Questions for Real Writing Practice:

- What elements play top roles when you plan teaching thematically, daily, semester-long, and yearly?
- Why should teachers make their own decisions?
- What are some strategies you have used (or experienced) successfully and some that have flopped?
- How do you balance structure and freedom in your classroom?

Academic Background for Vocabulary Concepts

The study of words is important in all our disciplines. There are three 'tiers' identified for academic vocabulary. The first tier consists of conversational words, like 'dude', and 'good' and are not worth spending much time on in the classroom. I taught a whole lesson on ways to replace 'good' in writing because I was taught that 'good' isn't a descriptive enough word. Now, we all know, if said right, it can express anything from disdain to intense satisfaction but on the page, it isn't enough. It was replaced with awesome, fantastic, groovy and other double-rainbow words. The second tier goes to the more scholarly words that play a role in higher-level comprehension. Daniels and Zemelman (2014) suggest we spend most of our efforts here because these words are the markers of literacy in a subject area. Then, there are the specialty words that have little overlap but are markers of a specific expertise. These should be less of a focus once the brain's ability to memorize useless details is established. The words on the third tier are quickly forgotten unless one is immersed in the lingo for personal interests or professional reasons. For example, I remembered every bone in the body for an anatomy exam, so I have proven that ability, but don't ask me to name any without time to study. We do not retain words that we do not use for long unless they spark our interest. Thus, I still know that phalanges are the tips of our fingers and toes, but don't know my vomer bone from my sacrum.

According to Daniels and Zemelman (2014) when we focus on academic vocabulary these should be our criteria for selection:

1. Importance and Utility—The word appears frequently across a variety of domains. These words, if understood in specific relationship to your content, enhance learning.
2. Instructional Potential—Students can use the new word to make connections and understand concepts.
3. Conceptual Understanding—The understanding of this word will provide precision and specificity in describing the concept.

These criteria align with the research, a summary of which is easiest to learn in bulleted format:

- The single most effective way to improve vocabulary is wide and regular reading
- Students learn more words when we focus on fewer words and provide multiple exposures
- Teaching context clues requires students to see relationships among words and make inferences
- Graphic organizers can promote an understanding of the complexity of words
- Make learning personal: When students use the words and feel ownership they are more likely to remember new vocabulary

- Make it transparent: model word-solving strategies for students, such as using context clues and word parts (prefixes, suffixes)
- Make it fun: Word play can spark a students' sense of discovery

Questions for reflection:

How many words do you think you know?

____

Helpful facts:

- The Oxford English dictionary lists 464 definitions for the word 'set', but it still only counts as one word.
- Receptive vocabulary words and expressive words both count. For example, I know what 'tertiary education' means when I read it, but I don't think I've ever used it in a sentence until this one. I'd still get to count it as a 'word' on my list.

The answer isn't the same for any two people and even the experts disagree on an average, but they do agree that the 'average' high school senior has around forty-thousand words.

Follow-Up Reflection Questions:

How do you choose the words that are given attention?

____

____

____

Real Writing Response:

I seek to expand my students' vocabulary only to the extent that it will help them be the best teacher possible in the classroom. Concepts are more important than words at our level but the common lingo is part of our culture of education so those are included in the dictionary. Teens believe that 87.5% of what we say is irrelevant and 12.5% is unreasonable. Like when we say, "be careful" as they ride off on wet pavement or "please pick up after yourself". You know, teacher things to say. No Fun. Boring. Teacher words can be carefully chosen to guide learning and they can be chosen to spark interest too.

List 5 of your favorite words. Consider both the connotations (feelings and judge-y meanings) and the denotations (actual meanings):

Example for connotation—the term for a yoga pose I do is 'supta baddha konasana'. If you replace this word with "frog-legged back stretch" it just doesn't sound as poetic. There are even negative connotations with the word 'frog-leg'; it reminds me a meal of these poor little fellows shared at a restaurant years ago where the phrase 'tastes like chicken' was oft repeated. We all have words we deem 'unacceptable' for the classroom, that are accepted in other contexts. My son was busted for saying 'and chill' after the teacher said "Netflix" before he knew what it really meant. This is a boy with some impulse control issues, also known as a teenager, and I explained clearly how singing a song aloud with the 'N-word' or 'Ho' in some contexts could be misconstrued. I know that he is singing along with a rapper, but the guy next to him on the subway may not. We teach a common language for awareness and we remind kids that the middle-finger is not acceptable, yet I have a teacher friend who posts pictures of herself flipping off the world. The N-word and 'Ho' are two on my list of 'no' words in class. "Please don't use that language" is repeated, nicely. That is what my son says too when I call someone 'thick'. I knew when my class gasped that "pissed" was not acceptable language in front of middle-schoolers and I knew when a friend told me "I wouldn't talk to my dog that way" that "edie-waa ship-sho" was a phrase in Korean I would not be teaching to others. Apparently, that has multiple meanings these days too and good communication of words and boundaries go both ways.

I don't have to deal with this at the tertiary level because we share an understanding of appropriate language in the classroom, and we are all adults. Only shared words are accepted in the classroom—or another language if you still need to transition to English. Or-ay e-way ould-cay eak-spay Ig-Pay Atin-Lay. Or not, your choice. Those whose words are vulgar are not tolerated as part of 'polite' society. Some say that polite society is over-rated and antiquated, but I say it is a standard we should continue to strive towards for school. Politeness matters too, and words must be chosen with care.

List five words that little kids think are neat:

____

____

Real Writing Response:

My guess: pickle, boogers, dinosaurs, candy and Mom. In that order. Chances are you are not going to be able to keep from grinning at the answers that you get, and some may be hilariously inappropriate. Just keep it professional always in the classroom. And if someone says "ligma" is their favorite word just remind him or her that bad memes are not acceptable choices for the classroom. And, if they get you, because you explain that "ligament" is a sinewy connecting tissue between a bone and a joint, then pretend to never know what the reference was. The next chapter starts with the importance of taking a break. That is a favorite word of mine. As in 'you deserve a break' rather than 'gimme a break.'

Learning Moment:

The words we select for our classroom naturally include an absence of words too because at some point most words start sounding like noise when we need a break. Make sure when you ask for it there is no whine in your voice. Wait a minute, at ten-thirty at night you can demand one. From who? Any self-imposed deadline looming other than survival responsibilities. Time to change into jammies. No more words for now.

Academics for Cooperative Learning

Hendrix (2008) writes of 'engulfment' and 'abandonment' as our childhood traumas; this psychologist recognizes that all people, not just those who experience dysfunction, feel the push and pull of interaction. It is healthy to push away at times and healthy to pull close at times. This is the nature of cooperation in our society. There are times when it is vital for survival and aides in learning and there are times when it is a distraction because, ultimately, only we can change and learn for ourselves. That doesn't mean we need any alone time to learn to ride a bike or swim. Cooperation is about the times when learning is best done as a social activity. It is needed in all classrooms, whether you assign groups or not. It is needed for two to work together or two thousand, not that I'm advocating those kinds of numbers for a classroom.

If cooperation were easy, then the divorce rates would lower, wars would cease, and conflict would be eradicated. The answer to many questions in education is collaboration. Despite years of working in groups and with partners, cooperative learning was not analyzed as a strategy for teaching until after my undergraduate experience. It was 'all the buzz' in the early 1990s so I attended three workshops that continue to influence my approach to cooperation in the classroom. These are the foundational elements:

1. **Interdependence:** This can be difficult to establish in our competitive society but if you want a group to interact well the members must take responsibility for the group's progress. A sense of interdependence is best built in balance with the next element.

2. **Individual Accountability:** Cooperative learning does not work if any member of a group does not understand their role in the process and agree to a common mission. Each person must take responsibility for a fair share of the work of learning to make progress.

3. **Interaction:** Cooperation requires interaction skills that are developed in accordance with the maturity-level of the students. Those who teach online know that cooperation occurs every day in new and innovative ways without being face-to-face, but the screen can't be the only one teaching it. We know this from psychology and the monkeys, remember? Those who do not get contact with others of our species become dysfunctional. We all vary in how much interaction we need.

4. **Interpersonal and Social Skills:** To build trust one makes choices that help rather than harm the group's progress. How to offer kind feedback and support one another must be taught if the students do not come to the lesson with that prior knowledge.

5. **Group Processing:** Take time to process both the interactions and the results. Awareness and feedback are necessary to become independent learners and that continues to be valued, even within a cooperative situation. The balance of self and others is easiest in a non-stress situation. These two questions could prompt the processing:

- What did you see happening that was positive?
- How could we improve our cooperative learning?

There are many options for utilizing cooperative learning skills once these elements are established. Two ways include assigning roles in a learning situation and modeling the elements when working with the 'whole-class' group or as a 'fishbowl' for processing the details of how to interact. The roles assigned depends on the goals of the lesson and the content. To determine the roles you assign, consider the objective. If you want a debate, the roles can be different than if you want a brainstorming session. If the goal is cooperation, then playing with all kinds of roles can help students understand what it means and give students a variety of experiences:

- Writer/Listener/Reader/Speaker: These are needed for any literacy-based cooperative learning activity, in no specific order. Schools sometimes prioritize reading above the rest; it is time to recognize the equality of each.
- Questioner/Summarizer/Visualizer/Predictor/Connector /Synthesizer: When the elements of proficient reader research are engaged then learning is more likely to occur. Mix and match, just like at Taco Bell.
- Adder/Subtractor/Multiplier/Divider: If numeracy is the goal then these basics could work. For more advanced mathematics maybe Computer/Steps Reminder/Recorder/Checker.
- Critic/Contempt-er/ Defender and Stone-Waller: If apocalypse is on the agenda, these are your horsemen. Since I've never planned an apocalypse I have never used those four roles in the classroom, but I could see 'similar' roles for a good debate.
- Ace/King/Queen and Jokester: If you want to play cards, these are the ones. Otherwise I cannot imagine a need for a jokester role. The clowns can come out to play in any configuration but trying to 'require' humor in a group could be awkward.
- Sniff/Scurry/Hem and Haw: If you want to find cheese or adapt to changes. These four don't actually work

together to find the cheese. Scurry and Sniff (two mice) rely on instincts rather than reason to run off and find their cheese and the two humans work independently because change must happen from within. They write on the walls of the maze for each other but do not read the writing on the walls. (Johnson, 1998)

- President/House Representative/Senator/Judge: If you want to create a democratic system based on our study of the possibilities at the time.
- Observer/Researcher/Hypothesizer/Conductor/Analyzer /Concluder: If you want to engage in the scientific method.
- Drummer/Guitarist/Lead Vocalist/Keyboards: If you want to start a rock-n-roll band.
- Pooh/Kanga/Eeyore/Tigger: If you want to examine someone's prior knowledge of the hundred-acre woods.
- Mr. Know-It-All/Sir Pompous/Miss Monopolizer/Queen Loudmouth: The team I would least like to accompany on a road-trip. But, once I got to know them I might label them Mr. Caring, Sir Misunderstood, Miss Observant and Queen of the One-Liner. The chemistry of any group can change with under or over-exposure. Which is why most of us stick with the next set of roles.
- The generic "leader/presenter/time-keeper & general task-master/recorder" can often work for getting the work done, but with some imagination your roles can be developed with your learning goals in mind. Just don't make the roles more complicated than need be and explain what each role entails.

Stories of positive cooperation surround us, from the Wright Brothers to the slaves building the pyramids of Egypt, to that aunt and uncle who stayed married for thirty happy years, as far as any of us could see. They cooperated, or they died. Modern life requires less cooperation for survival than at any time in the past. It is up to us to determine how to teach students what cooperation looks like in our classroom. It is a skill modeled and learned throughout life, whether you are a slave trying to survive or a brother hurtling through the great blue yonder. The skill of cooperation is how we survive, as a civilization. The role of a teacher involves learning and modeling how to interact in all kinds of situations.

Question for Reflection:

How do you determine the right time to use cooperative learning, the size of the group, and the roles?

____

____

____

____

____

____

____

____

Real Writing Response:

I rode my bike alone early with my training-wheels scooting over the dirt and Fang trotting along beside me, but I was supported. We exist in cooperative units, families and classrooms and societies that constantly change so the question of timing, number, and role is an interesting one to explore. The time to use interactions depends on our goals and the lessons we teach. That varies and is as subjective as the determining of roles.

Teachers roles change from expert to coach to social-worker to psychologist depending on the situation and that's just in a few minutes in the classroom. We all know the complications of roles and cooperation from our own experiences.

Kagan (2013) suggests that the 'ideal' group has four members. One 'top', two 'mid-tier' and one 'low'- level student. The criteria for the labels was subjective, but I tried this once or twice using students' grades in class to determine their level. It worked well except for Dietrich, and we all know a Dietrich or two. I still often use Kagan's suggested four members and roles because it is a good size group for sharing and discussing and the tables in my class are conducive to quartets. The numbers in our cooperative groups constantly morph and so there is no 'ideal' number. There are cooperative learning situations where four is ideal and others where two is the only viable option and times when Dietrich makes it impossible until you figure out how to get him to collaborate.

Two of the best groups of six that I know have recently lost members. I am the baby of an immediate family of six that lost its mother and father this year. That story is too complicated to tell here. As is your family's story too, most likely. The other group is six neighborhood friends who've been close since kindergarten. They are three sets of brothers who vacationed, camped, played hide-and-seek, caught fireflies, jumped on trampolines, played Airsoft and watched countless movies together. There were others included. They are all well-rounded young men with sports-friends and girlfriends and band-friends and such, but this group of six is tight-knit.

This summer they sailed a raft on the Cass River. The cooperative learning required for this task was like any classroom project, but the stakes were high. No one voluntarily goes for a swim in the Cass. Trust had to be strong because anyone on the raft could easily tilt it and soak them all. The roles ranged from captain to support crew to paddlers, but they rotated and negotiated and did it all without help from the adults. We've been side-lined, made superfluous by their cooperation.

Ben has been one-sixth of this family of friends for thirteen years. He will still be a part, but as a freshman at Colby he is too far away to visit until Christmas. Five of his close friends (and one brother) are sitting in my television room trying to decide what movie to watch. They probably miss Ben's wisdom and level-headed-ness, along with his wit and smile. So, bittersweet are these days of teenagers leaving the home and the nest being swept away by the weathering of time. Home is not a place for me. It is people. Family. Friends. Tribe. Whatever you call them, learning to cooperate with them starts at home and continues throughout life. School is an important place to try out various roles and groups for varying amounts of time so that students can learn in as many situations as possible. It cannot effectively replace family, but it is a support network for children to learn about socialization and content-areas that may spark an interest in higher pursuits.

Learning Moment:

With careful planning and frequent implementation, the groups at your school can learn from each other. Whether the cliques are Nerd/Jock/Burn-Out/Bandsie, Greaser/Soc, Crips/Bloods/Wet-Back Power, Farmers/Townies or any other combination of people, the way to move beyond stereotypes is to collaborate with those outside one's group. In the US we are an individualistic society that values family and that also holds individuals personally accountable for their community. This practice is most valuable if the students are taught to cooperate with even the Dietrichs. And the Dietrichs are taught to work with everyone else. Working collaboratively means different roles outside the classroom are melded with 'learner' inside the classroom walls.

Academics for Graphic Organizers

Graphic organizers have been shown to improve problem-solving communication, critical and creative thinking, argumentative writing and vocabulary acquisition (Allen, 2007; Marzano, Pickering & Pollock, 2012; Zollman, 2011). The visual representation of ideas helps students to remember the material and the relationships between the concepts. Graphics help build the schema that is crucial for learning.

Question for Reflection:

How do you match content with the 'right' graphic?

____

____

____

____

____

____

____

____

____

Real Writing Response:

Pictures are worth a thousand words, and this one is a favorite of mine. I thought it may work for my son's senior photo, but that picture cannot contain animals and clearly a red-feathered bird has landed on his head. Strike one, this is not the correct graphic for the situation.

Strike two, it cannot contain legs either, so this isn't the correct graphic for the job.

Story Impressions are a way to capture students' interests and test their prior knowledge that combines the research on "predicting" with a creative writing exercise, but it is not a graphic. The prompts are key words and phrases from a reading or unit of study. For example, there are many words from the Department Dictionary section that are not in this text. For these words I will combine a *Story Impression* strategy with a graphic organizer for learning vocabulary. If the content I wanted to convey related to soccer or senior pictures, then this graphic could work. A photo can spark interest and a story just as easily as a word, depending on the kind of learners in your class.

I learned about Story Impressions during a professional development experience that included weekly meetings for two years. We learned strategies and then worked together as a team with two professors from Arizona State to implement our own Action Research projects and process the implementation of strategies. I studied Free-Voluntary-Reading (FVR) and learned that my class library needed to fit my students' reading-level more accurately. I also deduced this through observation as one second-language learner tried to read Moby Dick with a Spanish-to-English dictionary. I barely trudged through that one in my own language, so I felt her pain. I also studied the Story Impression and learned that students scored higher on vocabulary tests when this strategy was used rather than direct instruction.

Let's do it as an example. Here are some words from the dictionary to practice with:

- Bullying
- Victimology
- Closure
- Zone of Proximal Development (ZPD)
- Inclusion
- Heteronormativity
- Stereotype Threat

The directions for this activity are to include the words in a brief story in the order that they appear. I am going to do so in the next paragraph, so you may want to stop reading here and practice with the words above.

___

___

___

My story Impression:

Sometimes Pat likes **bullying** little children. But, they don't understand. She's not mean, just having a l laugh. Someone studying **victimology** might call her a woman with issues. They may ask if she needs **closure** on some childhood trauma. A teacher may say that Pat needs a test to determine her **Zone of Proximal Development (ZPD)**. They may encourage her to stay at least twenty feet away from young children if they didn't understand. Pat is an **inclusion** advocate and defender of innocence even if she bullies a bit. It isn't bullying to tell a little girl "don't you worry sweetheart, I'm taking you right back to Momma" and grin because she's played with her in the park for hours and wants a break. The fall off the rock left no scrapes, but the tears for Momma were a welcome excuse. Her Momma was busy though. The Momma's partner was a man, and **hetero-normativity** made Pat less likely to take the child to her father. She decided to break the **Stereotype Threat** and take the bundle of nap-needing fussiness to her Daddy instead.

The End.

Most of the graphic organizers I use in the classroom are designed specifically for the assignment and the one below is no different. Also, I'd like to apologize to all my nieces and nephews who I referred to as "birth-control" when I was a bully of a teenager. I never considered how hurtful that could sound and I will always love you. I was teasing; and five little children yelling in the kitchen as they climbed all over me did make me think about the commitment of parenting. I learned from their Grandpa who pretended he really didn't enjoy children unless they were old enough to sit around the campfire and tell stories. He also pretended to hate cats, but then he'd tickle and play with a kitten and we all saw the fib and the twinkle in his eyes. The graphic organizer below is designed because I was concerned about students remembering the wrong definition after completing a Story Impression.

How I used it:	**Word to Learn:**	**What it means:**
In my example teasing is mistaken for bullying; one becomes another if the people involved do not communicate clearly.	Bullying	My definition would be using your strength or position to get people to do what you want or to torment another.
In my example it is used to indicate that the study of what it is to be a 'victim' is complicated and often linked with gender issues.	Victimology	It is the study of the effects of being the victim of a crime. We empathize with the victims and the culprits at times, depending on our experiences. We all have complicated ideas about what it means to be a victim.

It is used to indicate a need someone may have after experiencing a traumatic incident.	Closure	A sense of resolution is not the same as closure in the classroom. So, this is a case where the common definition varies greatly from education.
In the story it is used to indicate that someone who is a bully to young children should keep their distance.	Zone of Proximal Development (ZPD)	The step from 'guided' to 'independent' in learning.
A cause that one advocates for if they believe in fairness and are not likely to be bullies. The outliers as part of the accepted is a beautiful theory.	Inclusion	Securing opportunities for students with disabilities.
Identified as a harmful practice because it makes anyone 'hetero' feel they are 'normal'. Except, who wants to be normal these days anyways?	Heteronormativity	Valuing heterosexuality over other kinds of sexuality.
Used to call attention to the stereotype that mothers are more nurturing and have instincts that make them superior parents.	Stereotype Threat	The idea that we align with the stereotypes others hold regarding us. So, should I stop loving Starbucks because it is such a stereotype?

Learning Moment:

The content gets to be king in secondary learning situations. Process matters because of its ability to increase understanding but the content determines the form of the graphics that will best help students learn to take note and use the information wisely.

Chapter 6: Why make lessons relevant and fun?

Sometimes 'fun' is seen as too light a topic for serious consideration. The 'old song-and-dance' or the 'dog-and-pony-show' can be used to describe lessons that try to entertain. In addition, humor can take on forms that don't fit well in the classroom. Sarcasm, roasts, and irony can all be used in ways that belittle others. For these reasons teachers must use careful judgment to decide how and when to jest. For example, I roast a student who claims he is going to be the "only illiterate history teacher ever to graduate". When he asks if a school out West is taking applications I encourage him to apply and move out-of-state because "I really don't want illiterate teachers for my own children." The roast was deserved. With no disability form, homework completed, and a keen intellect, I knew he was teasing to start.

When I think of fun and teasing, I think of my father. Each year as we arrived at his home for Christmas Eve he'd joke about his contribution for making the meal we all knew Diane prepared. I grew up running the fields and pastures of my father's family lands and learned to love exploring the world through his example. It was with a heavy heart that I revised this chapter during the aftermath of his death. A funeral may not seem like the right focus for a chapter on introducing whimsy in the classroom, but it is relevant because he defined fun for my childhood. I made a mistake at my father's funeral though.

Jules sent Grandpa off with a wonderful roast. As did my mom, her grandma, from beyond the grave and many others. I read this instead of roasting:

A Poem for Dad

My dad was a Saturday night and a summer day all rolled into one

While Mom drove the Buick, he rode Darci's motorcycle

When Mom went to graduate school, he introduced me to fast food and fast cars

Great-grandchildren will remember him as a cowboy-boot wearing, gun-totin' legend

Who shot a rattle-snake from the back of his bucking bronc

I'll remember him as a polka-dancing expert who let me ride on his toes

Barn dances and campfire stories too numerous to tell swirl with my memories of Dad

He water-skied with me on his shoulders and sailed through the air over jumps

He dumped buckets of cold water on the backs of the bathing beauties

And got five skiers up at once behind our Jolly Roger

He taught me to sandbag in Euchre, spike in volleyball and that a perfect game is achievable

Howsomever, I will remember more than the fun

He taught me to get back on the horse over and over

"You're a Deneen, and Deneens are tough" was a mantra that got me through scrapes and heartaches

He was as protective as Fang in his own way, and much less likely to bite

Dad taught me to stand on my own while knowing that family and clan
Are willing to give you a ride on their shoulders now and then
And there's no reason not to make a request "while yer up"
While Mom was my rock, Dad gave us our wings
Edi-Wa-Ship-Sho, Dad, we've got a story to tell

I chose to read this graveside, hoping that the crowd would be more intimate, like the memorial for my mother a few months earlier. Instead, Dad's graveside was raucous, as are most Deneen gatherings. I wasn't ready to read aloud because the timing was terrible, as relative after relative whispered in my ear. My mother's death ten months earlier had no bearing on my Dad's death, they'd been divorced more than thirty-three years, but the kind words were true. Losing two parents in less than a year was difficult. The grieving relatives piled in from Washington, California, Hawaii, Flushing, and my brother re-routed from Spain to Michigan to be there. Jules's roast was bittersweet with jokes about laughing around the campfire and tales of their mutual friend, Plugsie, who collapsed in a folding-chair and sent his spaghetti flying. You didn't have to be there to imagine the scurrying comforters and my dad, laughing and pointing.

My mom's roast was unintentional. My sister bought the flowers that sat next to his casket during the funeral out of funds left by our mother. This included the flowers labeled "husband" even though his second wife of thirty years was the one to pick those out. I found the fact that my mom bought all the flowers for my dad's service hilarious. I imagined her laughing and pointing from some heavenly vista. Sometimes humor is slapstick, like the image of spaghetti in the air if no one gets hurt. Sometimes it is word-play like this old joke:

I read that a milk-bath can soothe dry skin, so I went around the corner to the dairy farmer. He asked, "do you want it pasteurized?" and I replied, "no, just past my bum, I can splash it up there."

Sometimes humor is light as a pun and sometimes it is complicated. I recently watched a comedian who quit on stage because she'd had enough of laughing at scarring childhood traumas. She still managed to do so for her final 'bit' but it was tense. Thus, if we can laugh at a funeral, our own faux paus, and childhood trauma, it is clearly acceptable to find ways to laugh and enjoy the classroom. We all see the value in laughter and sunshine, even if what causes it can be dark at times. Laughter and fun are good for us, even if pain is sometimes the hidden, or not so hidden, source.

The mistake I made at the funeral was unrelated to the roast. It involved secret-telling. My cousin shared her mom's story of teen-pregnancy and shotgun-wedding shame. To which I responded, "Really, you'd think since your dad went to prison for armed robbery after using my dad's gun for the heist, she would have more perspective on what she considered shameful." I did not know that cat wasn't yet out-of-the-bag, so to speak. Or maybe the story my dad told me wasn't true. He was known as a bit of a tall-tale teller. The point is, not everyone is going to think you're funny. In those instances, it's best to smile, nod and move on with the lesson. We aim to engage in the classroom without it shocking the audience, and we have little control over what students find fun or funny. Let the crickets chirp, but don't continue to fill the space if your audience isn't attuned. Listen to the crickets and find ways to build harmony. After a long, blank stare my cousin and I turned the conversation back to lakeside memories as though I'd never uttered a word.

The teen years are a complicated mix of learning without much of the big-picture perspective that comes with experience. Nothing is written in stone, and our ideas of fun vary greatly but we can enliven lessons by asking interesting questions, including breaks, games, competition, challenges, and by figuring out what motivates each group or even each student if the numbers are low. These possibilities for infusing the classroom are considered in this chapter:

- Music
- Games
- Competition
- Clubs and Workshops

These are just some of the ways a challenge helps to motivate students. We may be engaged because we care deeply about passing and the teacher barely speaks English, but if we can just pass this one more math class at the community college then our dream of being a book-nerd or an astronaut can be realized. We may be engaged because the teacher is enthused, and his field-trip involves taking thirty sixth-graders in a small plane to fly over town. Yes, we piled into aircraft at the local airstrip. I can't imagine the paperwork or the justification that would require; we sat two to a seat because we were pint-sized. We may be engaged because the embarrassment of a misstep at the halftime show frightens marchers almost as much as the naked-at-school-nightmare of first-day jitters. Fun matters for learning and is a wonderful option for sparking engagement in so many academic contexts.

Discussion Questions for Real Writing Practice:

- What would you do with two free hours to fill in a learning situation?
- How are you involved with music, games, competition, clubs or workshops?
- What are some relevant ways you can include fun for learning?
- What is a whimsical moment you could share with students?

Academics of Music

Brewer, C. (1995). *Music and learning.* Publisher unknown, city unknown. This is as far as I got trying to find academic support to 'prove' that we learn with music before I realized it doesn't need verified. We can safely say this without coming across as know-it-alls or dismissive of research because it is so universal that 7UP holds concerts for deaf people. The song can be as natural as a stream rushing over rocks; it can be pop, jazz, reggae, soul, blues, pumping beats, country twang, the violin, opera, hip-hop or more; music moves us all. The connection between music and mathematics is firmly established and clear in history, English, foreign languages, and sound waves are studied in science. I learned line-dancing and square-dancing in PE and the music was essential. It played in the background of every art, shop or drafting class I attended and took center stage for the half-time show on Friday nights. It represents our national-pride to start the games too.

We know that music can soothe the savage beast and the musicality of communication can be applied to learning in situations ranging from campfire sing-alongs to algebraic equations. The ABC song and the ditties that make Jack and Diane memorable are related. Whether we rock out to The Wiggles, Neil Simon or Violent Femmes we realize that "fruit salad, yummy, yummy" is easier to remember than Carl Perkin's quote on rocks, "if it weren't for the rocks in its bed, the stream would have no song". Songs help us to memorize and they work with the brain to make the learning long-term.

The strategy that lends itself to manipulating music for a lesson is one we can call "Weird Al Goes Academic". It is an adaptation of Copy Text, a strategy that is constructed like a modified **cloze**. The students alter words and change the topic of a poem, quote, or song into a parody. I tried to create a rap example, but the pace was tongue-tying so songs about socks and rocks in a rap format were abandoned for a song to the tune of Buffalo Springfield's *For What it's Worth.* I wanted to start with the line "there's dumplin's happening here" but that got me craving Chinese food each time, so I went with the quote from Carl Perkins for content:

Rare music's happenin' here
Even crystals aren't exactly clear
There's a stream in the sun over there
Signing like nobody cares

I think it's rocks, people, that's the sound
You hear as it's flowing down

There's mad waves being thrown
Into the rocks water's blown
The cliffs are singing their lines
Booming down from heaven, for all times

I think it's rocks, hey, that' the sound
You hear as it's flowing down

Cut a path for the creek
A frozen river, high up in the peaks
Streaming along a' ferrying wine
Coastly sighs, hooray for outside

Crashing rocks, hey, that' the sound
You hear as it's flowing down

Water flows into the deep
Wind in your ears it will seep
The stars know when you're afraid
You dance in line, the wind come and blow you around

I think it's rocks, hey, that's the sound
You hear as it's flowing down

Music takes us places. If angry it allows release in a harmless avenue, excitement turns to dance, and gospel can lead to swaying. If we're figuring out how to turn poetry into lines, music can help us learn. Sometimes we just need to sing aloud whether it's in the shower or on stage or in the classroom choral reading. There are valuable ways to bring music into lessons ranging from background, to creative writing inspiration, to a strategy for learning. After writing this song I will never forget that rocks make the song of waves crashing and streams flowing. What this meant to the man who wrote songs for Elvis and Johnny Cash is open to interpretation. The creative exercises can spark our memory, as can songs like "conjunction, junction, what's your function?" from Saturday-morning cartoons years ago.

Question for Reflection:

How do you bring music into your classroom and link it to lessons?

____

____

____

____

____

____

____

____

____

____

____

____

Real Writing Response:

This strategy is a natural for me since I rarely get the lyrics right as I sing along to the radio. "Dirty deeds and they're done dirt cheap" became "dirty jeans and the dunder-chief" for twenty years, until Ryan pointed out that I was singing the wrong words. Loudly. I have been a quieter person for the past twenty years because my music collection was in flux and fluff often filled the radio-waves as our children grew. I can enjoy *Let it Go* and absolutely love campfire songs, but it's not the sort of music I'd download. My music collection was purged as the boys got old enough to ask, "What are the words?" and I realized that "head like a hole" and others were just not appropriate for minors.

Like most people, I love music and songs hold special significance for the various stages of my life. Childhood is represented by songs like "can't roller skate in a buffalo herd" by Roger Miller and ditties such as "the Cannibal king with the big brass ring, fell in love with the dusky maid, and every night by the mellow moonlight across the bay he'd wa-aye-ade. Baroomp, baroomp, baroomp diddly -oddy-aye". On my 'favorites' the oldies range from *King of the Road* by Roger Miller, *London Calling* by The Clash or *Le Nozze Di Figaro* by Mozart. The newest additions are *Sex and Candy* by Marcy's Playground and *Ho Hey* by the Lumineers. As iTunes replaced CDs, like albums, eight-tracks, cassettes, and Victrolas along the way, the music of each generation adds to the cacophony of choices.

Music changes fast and I took a few generations not keeping up with the trends. *Fruit Salad* was repeated ad nauseum when music went from rated R to G for me. Eminem took me back to PG with *Lose Yourself* and non-explicit versions of *Slim Shady*. Then Lady Gaga, Beyoncé, and Jason took us to the world of pop. Many stayed true, like some classic Bowie and Prince, and others shifted as tastes changed and new songs got sung around the campfire or played for dancing in the gym. "I got off the riverboat, in the spring of fifty-two, and walked into a gamblin' house, as gamblers often do-oo-oo-oo-ooh" made a reappearance this year in my life while trying to find appropriate funeral music, while *In my Feelings* by Drake plays in the background as I write. Most can relate to an eclectic mix of music through the decades.

I have let students bring in and share school-appropriate music. One brought *If I Die Sudden* by John Mellencamp for its shock value. The line "put me in a pine box, six feet underground" tickled his fancy. Another brought in *Diamonds on the Soles of Her Shoes* for the upbeat tempo and the words to the song. James' favorite was Indigo Girl's *Closer to Fine* while Ryan would pick *Awwsome!* No, that is not a typo. Shy Glizzy spells the word with two W's and an exclamation point and it is not close to classroom appropriate. A neighborhood senior listed it in his interview as a 'pump-up' song for basketball and I believe this is its appeal to Ryan. That and the liberal use of the f-word.

We get that. It is generational and the reason that slang must keep changing so fast. Teens and tweens keep testing limits, so that anyone older must continually feel tragically un-hip. Which doesn't stop me from responding "drop top" when a student says, "rain drop" so I can discuss the reasons this song is not allowed in the classroom. Guiding students to analyze and critique while keeping it classroom appropriate requires listening to music and remembering that sex and drugs as a theme in music is older than rock-n-roll. That doesn't make misogyny or glorification of drugs and violence okay, it just means that cutting edge may be a little too sharp for classroom consideration.

Learning Moment:

As an English and ESL teacher I used songs to teach about cultures, decades, poetry, history, *Les Miserable*, and to stimulate creativity. I bonded over music with students through talent shows and choral readings and encourage expression in all its various forms if it is appropriate and not distracting from the lesson. I turned off the background music long ago as ideas started to flow that I did not want interrupted, but with headphones students can even listen and work. Music can provide the break, or it can boost the lesson, and both are valuable.

The Academics of Games

Games and chores have inhabited the classroom for as long as the idea of gathering together to learn has existed. Yet, the distinction between 'fun' and 'chore' is not as simple as it first seems. Lessons can go from enjoyable necessity to terrible inconvenience in the blink of an eye if rushed, confusing, or one's mood is deflated by a negative comment. The newness of peek-a-boo wears off and even "button-button-who's-got-the-button" with grandma eventually gets replaced with charades after dinner. The games that amuse us change over time and vary with culture, experiences and age all impacting the effectiveness.

Generally, students are going to find a way to have some fun and if it's part of the lesson it leads to learning rather than detention and resentments. Loud and quiet are relative in game-like settings too. If you plan to play games in the classroom, keep it safe, productive (mostly), and orderly. So, ironically, games rely on the academics of rule-setting.

Safety is about rules and Starbucks comes through again with a modern example. Truly, I get no kickbacks beyond refills if Joe is working. Employees got together to set these rules for their third-space concepts:

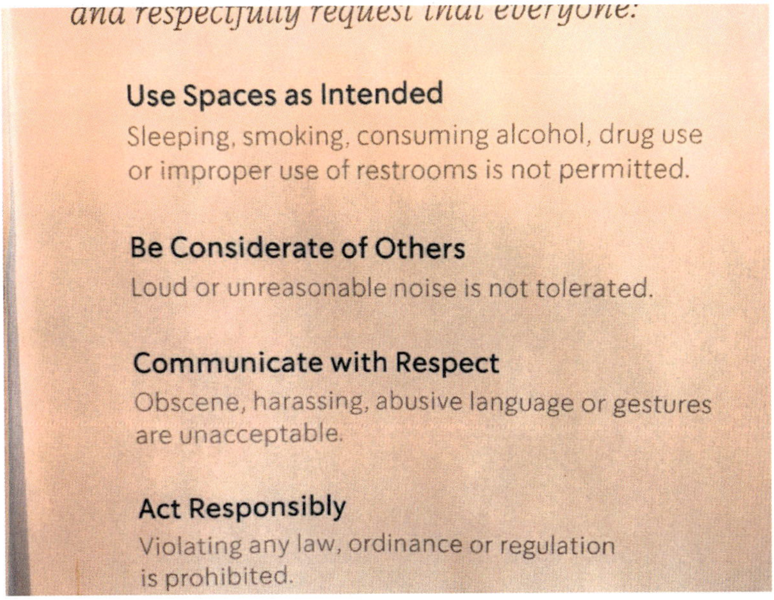

and respectfully request that everyone:

Use Spaces as Intended

Sleeping, smoking, consuming alcohol, drug use or improper use of restrooms is not permitted.

Be Considerate of Others

Loud or unreasonable noise is not tolerated.

Communicate with Respect

Obscene, harassing, abusive language or gestures are unacceptable.

Act Responsibly

Violating any law, ordinance or regulation is prohibited.

Within the boundaries set, learning-directed games can motivate and engage students in content lessons. While classroom rules can be general like these set by Starbucks and are often a collaborative effort, the rules for games require specificity and can be revised on-the-spot and recorded for future planning, based on experiences.

Question for Reflection:

When and why are games worthwhile in your classroom?

Real Writing Response:

Here's a fun word game:

What do these four words have in common?

- Angel
- Boot
- Bullet
- Spoon

Think! You have two minutes to answer the question:

____

____

Fun for you? Maybe you'd prefer acting it out? Or being asked to shoot one? It is fun for me because all four are mementos. Two were thoughtful gifts from a niece to commemorate the lives of my parents. The other two were household items that remind me of times past. I am not a nostalgic sort, but a trip down memory lane can be positive. A trip into the creative side can be too, or the meditative state, and all can be harnessed and focused to improve learning. Many of my games involve activity when possible because I see my students for long stretches of time. My teachers labeled me 'hyper-active' back-in-the-day so that may also play a part in why I prefer games that get everyone out of their seats.

Early school memories are as fleeting as the rest, but some jump to attention. The swinging gate in my kindergarten classroom and the monkey-bars I swung from day after day. The group chase of Sammy and the confusion of what to do once he was caught. At some point he wanted the kiss and we thought he was suffering from a rare disease called "cooties". We wrote "cootie power" all over our folders to protect from the evil. These were sensitive times with quick hurts and healing. When I reflect on games in school I think back to recess, attending sporting events, dances and after-school activities before I remember games in the classroom like spelling-bee competitions and fun reviews. I enjoyed school immensely for the social aspects and had the ability to make it fun even when the teacher wasn't necessarily trying to amuse.

I've rarely felt unsafe in school, but I do know that games can get out-of-hand. Andrea Lender bit my butt on the playground, but that was just awkward. Baring a behind to the teacher to guarantee no teeth marks would have been embarrassing enough, but she left the door open and another teacher stood outside to keep it official. It felt like overkill, but I mooned my teacher to prove I would not need shots and was back to playing on the slide shortly afterward. I am not a muffin-baking miracle worker but including games that encourage both competition and cooperation is possible in various forms with no danger of butt-biting unless one is dealing with extremely immature students running rampant.

In the beginning of my teaching career, I used a *Party Games and Activities* (1990) publication from Hallmark to design classroom instructions. We played 'snow-ball' spelling review by writing words on white paper and throwing them back and forth until the whistle blew and students quizzed each other. I even adapted one so that students wore clothespins on their sleeves and competed to collect them from others in class. Anyone who crossed his or her legs lost their clothespin and stood until they saw someone else cross a leg. Then that person got all the other person's clothespins and got to sit down. It was a silly game, unrelated to the story being read-aloud, but it was a way to make listening quietly fun while the content remained the focus. Although, in retrospect, it was probably more distraction than it was aide.

My first observed lesson as a practicing intern involved a religious middle-school classroom, a trash basket, desks moved, and students scrambling to shoot wadded paper in the trash-basket before the other groups, so they could answer the question, earning points for their team. It was chaotic, so I learned that middle-schoolers need more rules and calming games at times. I adapted and played a "when-then" game for years. Each student had notecards that said "when _______________ happens, then you say __________________ or do ______________________". Students listened closely for the clue that it was their turn to keep the chain going. This game was adapted from an activity that a speech teacher practiced with my students and it wasn't until later that the link with Total Physical Response (TPR, Asher, 1969), a strategy for language learning was established for why this activity worked for my students.

Example:

When someone turns out the lights and asks, "What is the capitol of Michigan?", then you clap three times and answer, "The capitol of Michigan is Lansing. What is the capitol of New Mexico?"

When someone claps three times and asks, "What is the capitol of New Mexico?", then you stand on one leg and answer, "The capitol of New Mexico is Santa Fe. What is the capitol of Massachusetts?"

Games with activity get classes warmed up. I use notecards and combine this with an activity where students list twenty concepts worth remembering from their research and then write questions that relate. Students refer to this game as "that musical-chairs thing" even though there is no music or chairs involved. We form a circle of desks and switch spots if we share answers to the question. Using one less desk than the number of students in the group guarantees that there is always one person left standing to ask the next question. Creating the list together means more overlap. The teacher can also say "scramble" and everyone must find a new seat. This rule gives the game more spontaneity.

The fly-swatter competition tests game-show potential which is fun for many also. Students write an 'easy' question on a green slip of paper, a slightly challenging question on a yellow slip of paper, and a difficult question on a red slip of paper. This can also be a wonderful time to teach students about breaking down essay questions if the age is appropriate. Teams each send a representative to the central fly-swatting table and those students compete to slap the fly and answer a question correctly to earn team points. The red questions are worth more than yellow or green.

Another game I play for term-review is an adaptation of "Steal-the-Bacon" from the old-school gym class. Groups are each given a list of words or phrases to divide equally amongst themselves. Only the person with the word or phrase that answers the question can leave their seat, so there is cooperative interdependence necessary too. I ask a question and the first person to get out of their chair and get a piece of play-bacon off a central table can answer to win points for their team. Adapting games to new groups each year is fun and challenging. I include bingo and more because games are a way to make learning active even if there is more to 'active learning'.

Learning Moment:

Students asked to bring a 'rock' to class listened to my clarifying lecture on what counts as a 'rock'. The students were joking so I clearly stated, "no diamonds or drugs should come to school". That's a lesson my college students don't need to hear to know, but they sometimes state names so that became a rule. Setting limits makes you a teacher, not a wet-blanket, no matter what the peers of all ages may try to pressure you into doing. I've always known that being armed is dangerous unless one is well trained and the same is true for games in the classroom. It's all fun and games until someone gets hurt, so set the rules clearly and let the games begin.

The Academics of Competition

Competition is the genesis of motivation, both intrinsic and extrinsic (Kohn, 1993). We compete against ourselves and those around us in the perpetual survival-of-the-fittest struggle. Siblings have rivalries and Adam and Eve probably competed to see who could throw the apple farthest. Since the first person said, "no, let's try it this way" competition and sportsmanship have been part of the milieu in education. It means we don't lie, cheat, steal others' work, or generally harass those playing a game. It encompasses knowing limits for trash-talking and involves codes that support a 'defending champion' more if they don't brag and underdogs are cheered most vigorously in many contests.

Games have evolved from throwing rocks, brutal sword battles and feats such as chariot racing to become less violent but the danger continues in sports such as ice-waterfall climbing and bull-fighting to name two. And, like the people playing them, they are likely to continue to change. Rugby could eventually replace American football, with its emphasis on brute strength intact but the forceful head-butting left off the field. 'Gladiator' competitions return in different formats, with more precautions as we evolve to value brains over brawn for some situations and brawn over brains for others. Watching and taking part in competitive events is a large part of the school setting whether it is tennis, cheer, Ping-Pong, grades, stocks-and-commodities trading or perfecting dance moves. Teaching students to compete with honor and integrity is part of introducing sportsmanship at school. Even collecting rocks can be turned into a competition as evidenced by the value of diamonds, and the need for sportsmanship is evidenced by the proliferation of blood-diamonds.

The classroom is no retreat but study after study confirms that slowing down our minds and physical activity are both good for health, which is why extracurricular activities at school deserve to be considered a spot to develop literacy through socialization. Communication on the field is of significant value. Skills are required to navigate successfully, and sports competitions give schools and coaches the chance to develop young minds while the physical activities develop strong bones and muscles; a definite win-win situation for competition.

Question for Reflection:

What does sports-person-ship mean to you and what do we learn from competition?

____

____

____

____

____

____

____

Real Talk Response:

My husband and I were out for a walk along Lake Michigan. We were awed by the clouds rolling across the lake and watched the big black clouds and funky lightning patterns for a few minutes before realizing that we needed to take shelter. We walked fast and jogged before reaching the post office where we took cover. The rain was pounding, and we watched as a large sign across the road was torn down and slammed into a truck. The power wavered and went out. The post office dimmed but the generator across the street brought flickering light and we decided to call the boys to let them know we were settling in to wait out the storm.

The phone rang. And rang. And rang. Phone service is weak up north, so we sent a text. Still no response. Have you seen the joke about what parents think when you don't answer your phone?

What parents think when you don't answer your phone:

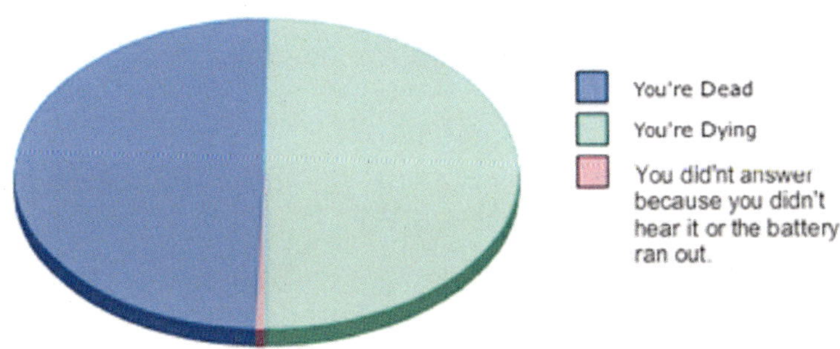

GraphJam.com

Well, as you can imagine, with the storm and the power-outage we got worried.

It is three-quarters of a mile from downtown Empire to the cottage. Uphill. We ran as fast as we could. The trees all seemed to be leaning sideways. The rain turned hard, like BBs. The thunder crashed right on top of the lightning. Trees and telephone poles and wires were all blown down. My lungs burned, and I ran wildly – dodging wires and trees that seemed ready to crash down at any moment. It took me five minutes to dodge tree-limbs and lightning strikes and make it to safety. It took my husband four and he and both sons were inside by the time I got there. I stood on the porch and was thankful for our safety rather than cursing my second-place finish. That is the essence of sports-person-ship to me. We cheer on our teammates and care more about a well-run race and personal bests than other matters.

And we're better at it than you. Oh yeah, roasted. Oops, my sports-person-ship slipped a bit there. What are we better at in Frankenmuth? Super-fandom. We won the award for "Battle of the Fans" and continue to out-cheer our opponents at sporting events. Competition can bring out the best and the worst in people.

Ryan dressed as a super-fan on neon night:

Sports-person-ship means the age at which it is okay to heckle is directly proportional to the age of the players. I could even insert a graph here to demonstrate but we can visualize the arrow pointing up to the right-hand corner of the page. The horizontal-axis labeled "age of student" and the vertical labeled 'level of jeering acceptable". No such graph exists because each person sets his or her own standards based on prerogative and the situation. My family was slightly appalled at the chant of "Adam let the whole team down" when we watched State take on their top rival in a soccer match. College players are accustomed to harsh words from the sidelines, depending on the game, but this was personalized to hurt the goalie's feelings and sung repeatedly by a large fan section for State. Heckling is more accepted with older contact sports, like those that descended from watching the lions kill Christians or maybe cock-fighting. It ranges from the sad little bleat of "mwwaaa-mwaaa-mwaaa" in a plaintive baritone after a foul or interception, to jazz-hands behind the backboard, to the coach who yells and throws chairs across the court. The general cheering and heckling atmosphere at many sporting events muddles issues of what it means to be a good competitor.

Sports like American football and European football are related, but one is deemed 'safer' than the other in our household. Both can involve trash-talk, injuries, and muddy cleats but one is being researched hard in relation to brain injuries. Wear a helmet, seatbelt, and protect your head are the mantra of a generation that aged without seatbelts or helmets, but hindsight makes it clear. Ryan calls it 'hypocrisy' and I call it 'caution' and there is no competition because I am the adult.

Ryan is in the basement pounding on a punching bag, drenched in sweat. He is upset because we said he could play football once he was older and then new studies were released, and we decided that it was not safe. "You promised" is met with, "before we had all the information." The brutality of contact sporting matches – football, boxing, mixed-martial arts, etc. – are not encouraged in my family. Two footballers told me they aren't allowing their son to play either because their old injuries still plague them. I don't want to watch or be involved in any sport involving minors where sideliners growl and yell and coaches swear or worse.

Another reason not to allow Ryan to play football is his all-out nature. This is a kid who flew into a basketball-pole and knocked out a tooth on the playground. A moment that stands out for him in soccer is from an away-game where the other team's fan section was rowdy and loud and his move on the field silenced their cheers. His first 'quiet the crowd' moment counted more than goals for him. He doesn't need any 'give it one-hundred percent' speeches and is repeatedly asked to 'slow down' instead. The hegemonic masculinity, the weak-knees or the personality of the individual were not enough of an excuse though.

My husband had a wonderful football experience with coaches who cared and teammates who became friends for life. The hegemonic masculinity we could handle and is outweighed by the benefits and positive lessons sports can provide. It can be countered with a model who is caring and kind, and vetting of coaches. Nothing negative to be said about the football coach and yet still we changed our minds. Why? We didn't want our sons involved in a sport increasingly linked to brain degeneration. When they were young we said "yes" to playing in middle or maybe high-school but the reports continue to confirm our suspicions: football kills brain cells. We all only have so many of those to spare if we want to stay quick-witted and fleet of foot enough to survive. Is brain-injury possible in soccer or basketball or track? Absolutely, as it is possible playing on the playground, but that is a bet we are willing to take. It's also possible jumping off a bridge. Those are also not cheered unless the bridge is the right height and the water is clear.

Learning Moment:

Strength and speed and quick-wittedness have been revered since the dawn of time, whether they are attributed to natural selection or bestowed by the moon goddess. Early humans had to adapt or be the sacrifice or lunch. Students often waver between feeling bulletproof and easily shattered during the teen years. The many benefits to your health and chances to learn true sportsmanship in school-related events means extracurricular activities are a large part of learning in places where students are valued. For some that means quieting the crowd while others wish to get them revved. Socialization requires communication and sports-person-ship is the language of the lessons we teach on the field and anytime we coach a student towards growth beyond the classroom walls.

Academics for Workshops and Clubs

The workshop approach of Nancie Atwell (1998) can increase engagement because students decide what to read and write and the components are useful for multiple teaching venues and topics. The parts are as follows and are adaptable to any learning that is a process, which includes most forms of communication:

1. **Mini-lesson** (~10 minutes): A brief lesson about procedures, craft, or conventions. The topics for these are determined by the content needs and interests of the students.
2. **Status-of-the-class report** (~5 minutes): Each student checks in to tell the class what s/he will work upon during the workshop, while the teacher writes observational notes on students' charts, if a teacher is guiding the class.
3. **Writing/conferencing time** (~35 minutes): During this time students engage in any stage of the writing process while the teacher monitors and conferences with individual students who seek attention or appear to struggle. Probing questions are used to prompt improvements and reflection.
4. **Whole-class conference** (~10 minutes): The class is called back together, and students share finished pieces to 'publish' or ask for whole-group feedback.

Harvey Daniels' (2002) Literature Circles allow for student choice in his book-club approach that involves the following roles for small-group discussions:

Discussion Director: Your job is to develop a list of questions that your group might want to discuss about the reading. Don't worry about the small details: your task is to help people talk over the big ideas and share their reactions. Usually the best discussion questions come from your own thoughts, feelings, and concerns as you read.

Illustrator: Your job is to draw a picture relating to the reading. It can be a sketch, cartoon, diagram, flow chart, or stick-figure scene. You can draw a picture of something that is discussed specifically in your book, or something that the reading reminds you of, or a picture that conveys any idea or feeling you get from the reading. Any kind of drawing or graphic is okay– you can even label things with words if that helps. One at a time, group members get to speculate what your picture means, to connect the drawing to their own ideas about the reading. After everyone has had a say, you get the last word: tell them what your picture means, where it came from, or what it represents to you.

Summarizer: Your job is to prepare a brief synopsis of the reading. The other members of your group will be counting on you to give a quick (one or two minute) statement that conveys the gist, the key points, the main highlights, the essence of the reading. This role isn't done once the summary is completed though, because there are often discussions that deserve a summarizing end-cap to move the group along.

Literary Luminary: Your job is to locate a few special sections of the text that your group would like to hear read aloud. The idea is to help people remember some interesting, powerful, funny, puzzling, or important sections of the text. You decide which passages are worth hearing and then jot plans for how they should be shared. You can read passages aloud yourself, ask someone else to read them, or have people read them silently to discuss.

Vocabulary Enricher: Your job is to be on the lookout for a few especially important words in the reading. If you find words that are puzzling or unfamiliar, mark them, and then later jot down their definition, either from a dictionary or some other source. You may also run across familiar words that stand out– words that are repeated a lot, used in an unusual way, or key to the meaning of the text. Mark these special words too and be ready to point them out to the group. When your circle meets, help members find and discuss these words.

Connector: Your job is to find connections between the reading and the outside world. This means connecting the reading to your own life, to happenings at school or in the community, to similar events at other times and places, to other people or problems that you relate with the reading. There are no right answers here– whatever the text connects you with is worth sharing. Then ask, "so what?" and try to use your connection to increase understanding of a scene or concept.

Both the writing workshop and the book-club format are useful for aligning classroom plans with real-world options. The general mood of a gathering around a campfire is rare within school walls, but attainable in some clubs and workshops.

Question for reflection:

What do you do to bring a 'workshop' or 'club' feeling into your school setting?

____

____

____

____

____

____

____

____

Real Writing Response:

The clubs I've been involved in include theater, National Honor Society, school newspaper, foreign-exchange students, yearbook, running, dancing, drumming, nature, New Americans, book clubs, writing and more. I could equally enjoy a rowdy bike club and a silent meditative retreat. Neither would be my choice for two free hours though if I were queen-bee for a day.

If I got to run a club for two hours a week I know just how I would organize it. The first hour would follow the traditional workshop format with a brief mini-lesson, a status-of-the-class chart, time for conferencing, researching, reading and writing, and then a 'publishing' session where progress is recorded and reported as we consider what to focus on for the next session. The group size would remain low, because feedback for large groups is overwhelming unless classmate's input is highly valued.

The mini-lessons would guide us to provide valuable feedback, edit, revise, and fact-check or research. When I included a workshop format in a Montana classroom the students turned in so many pages of science-fiction and poems for me to read that I couldn't keep up, so parameters would need established. The mini-lessons would adapt to meet the needs of the group and content standards.

The second hour would be yoga. Work first, play later is the generally accepted mode but few in my workshop would consider literacy work either. Yoga and literacy can both be as much work as you decide. This tenet might be stressed at another brief mini-lesson to transition away from writing and sharing and intellectualizing. If the transition is made smoothly and positively the next hour can be devoted to yoga. The transition is the kicker sometimes.

Most of the yoga mini-lessons would center on these main tenets:

- Quiet
- Strength
- Breathe
- Balance
- Flexibility
- Intention

The status-of-the class would be a silent stretch time where students are reminded to "listen to your body, more than your mind", followed by a twenty-minute video where a Boho beauty takes us through the basics. This would be followed by ten minutes of floor poses, ten minutes of standing poses and fifteen minutes of final relaxation with an optional aromatic head-massage.

Unfortunately, the extracurriculars I was assigned to start did not stem from my interests. Instead I said "yes" when asked to put on school plays, run the National Junior Honor Society, and coach softball because it increased my likelihood of being hired. My prior knowledge involved painting scenery and standing in the outfield, not directing or coaching. The first play we put on had terrific sets, but no one remembered their lines. The second play had terrific sets and a loud crinkling noise stage-left as I prompted the play from the side-line. The third play involved skits and went off without a hitch. It was adorable, finally. The proof of success was that for three years in a row the numbers in Drama Club grew. I was basically running an after-school day-care for over fifty children single-handedly and we enjoyed learning together. The plays entertained the crowd no matter the level of performance because it was all family and friends.

The closest to a yoga club I ever got was Wilderness Club in the desert. We took teens to the mountains to ski and see snow for the first time. We traveled to Catalina Island and snorkeled with sharks and touched marine-life as we learned about marine biology. We took a back-packing trip to desert mountains that sang with birdsong and laughed at stories around the campfire. The simplicity of singing together around a campfire is more likely with a club that allows us to explore the world beyond the classroom walls. The magic of a campfire is not an option in school, but clubs can build community beyond the classroom doors to feed students' interests and make learning fun.

Learning Moment:

I do yoga with a small group of women, writing workshop with five friends, and book-club with around twenty. Ruth runs the book-club with humor, dog stories, and an obsession with Mahjong. I learn new books to read each month and love listening to the stories that range from how to prepare for a zombie apocalypse to how one woman feels she knows the author after reading a memoir. No one is in charge for the small writing group where I focus on fiction to make it a break rather than an extension of work. I have read and heard terrific stories about Vietnam, children in Africa, dogs, family, and more. My yoga sessions get my heart thumping and my muscles stretched. My imagination paints a more beautiful image than the reality which sometimes involves crying, swaying, and bean dip, but workshops and clubs are an ideal worth aiming for in terms of engagement for students, in class and out.

Chapter Seven: The future of literacy

I was floating along so peacefully, enjoying a Coke on a sweaty-hot summer day and dragging my toes languidly in ways to create ripples but not wakes. The motor of the boat cut out and the tension in the ski-line went slack so that I drifted between a swan and her offspring. They're called 'cygnets' rather than goslings so that wildlife experts have the terminology to distinguish. I was wearing a bikini and holding a bottle as I slid off the tube and glided in to the water to hide. I'd been dunked so many times as a child that I knew how to slip smoothly into the water without a ripple or the need to flip off the captain. He knew I got him. So, years later, don't judge me when you see me dunking Dad in the lake. He dunked me and picked me up and threw me screaming through the pool. He heard shrieks of laughter and that was it, for the most part. In the river that day there were no shrieks heard, but plenty of laughter and compliments on my ability not to spill the Coke.

My mother glided along and smiled as she emerged from the dunkings that came her way too. She never even put up a fuss, being the trooper that she was. We were a rowdy trio at the pool. She loved the water, so her poem focused on that. I read it aloud for her and my family and I share it here as a reminder that the future of literacy is firmly rooted in the learnings of the past.

A Prayer for Shirley

My mother taught me to be faithful to family. I was considered equal to my siblings, a diverse bunch if ever there was one. What we share is love and the conviction that we were equal in her eyes. If I am equal to my sisters and brother then I can also equal Shakespeare or Einstein or the homeless man at McDonalds, asking for money and getting a meal and some free lessons most likely. Mom taught me that better off didn't mean better than.

She taught equality and balance. She taught that basic needs should be met with security before more is considered and that charity is more than sending a check. She taught me that second homes are a sound investment and that time is more important than money. Her lessons ranged from the mundane, such as correcting me by saying, "Karen and I are going to the game, not me and Karen," to the profane, such as the importance and way to laugh at oneself. "Yes, very funny Debbie," was said sincerely even if my joke about her not going to the game was somewhat lame. Being nice was important even in humor, and Mom mostly liked to laugh at a good story. Or a squirrel antic. Or herself quite often.

One afternoon Brian, James, Ryan and I came down to help Mom with some plantings. She had fun telling about how she'd fallen into a bush and popped right back up but left an imprint in the front hedge. Sure enough, she pointed it out and laughed as we planted flowers together. It was the best sound, like a Caci giggle, and it will never be silenced if we keep learning our lessons and laughing together.

Complete knowledge was her view of heaven. No more doubts or questions. She deserves that and more. Thank you, Mom, for giving me the faith to believe in my own ability to forge a path. If I can be equal then I could even equal you, someday. You make me want to be a better person. Not better than others, but better than any earlier version of myself.

Mom taught me the importance of community and building it in whatever circumstances we find ourselves. She never moved far, but she continually made new friends. Mom taught me how to be a good friend. And when to turn out the *lights and hide and when to answer the door with a firm "sorry, not interested" if necessary.*

I can barely believe she's no longer here to observe, listen, and offer feedback. If asked. Or not, depending on the situation. Like a good friend.

She also taught me the value of being quiet, which I'll do now. And listening. And reading. Hydration too and eating my vegetables. And love, most of all. Thank you, Mom, Amen.

This was all I planned to read aloud at her memorial but after a pause, and the loving support I get from family but do not take for granted, I finished with this:

A Poem for Grandma

Just return me to the water

I understand

Whether the water is reincarnation; born again or the breaking of

Childbirth to a mother

Or the Ganges to the Hindu

or the sea

or the lapping beach on the shores of Lake Superior

Actually, recant that

Be sure the water is warmer than Superior with its

Cold and frozen ways

But not hot lava

Or both

Because we must understand the extremes

To achieve balance

We must have life and death

But She will wait for the soft rain

Already ashes

Not yet dust

Her spirit may lift quickly, or it may linger

But it will rise

Through families and the words

And the grandchildren and the spirit

We understand

Return to the water

Only when ready to cry

The sun through clouds and silver-linings will remain

And balance beauty with grace and understanding

Let go of the grief and embrace a new day

Soon, but remember the lessons and the love too

Show your appreciation by loving the world

Care

Be a positive loving force in the battle for good

But avoid conflict

Seek happiness because it is what you deserve

As does your family and friends and strangers

Consider yourself equal

Worthy

Through virtue and hard work

Why not cheat?

Because then you don't learn

Why not quit?

Because then you don't learn

Education is the root of life

So, understanding is important

When I die...return me to the water please

Oh yeah, be polite...She taught us that one too

And kind to animals and non-judgmental

And also not to worship false idols or stress out.

What you're doing right and wrong

Let it go

And let me fly

Maybe the air too...or the Earth

Do with me what you will

I understand

When the world looks back at the dawning of the digital age it may be with contempt or scorn or maybe it will be with reverence and awe. Most likely neither, because those generations will also be focused upon looking ahead and will see the mistakes of the past more clearly, but we can hope ours can be a time of progress. The new global world is upon us and to participate we cannot isolate ourselves and ignore it. Onward, ho.

Is the future best met head-on or with your back turned? Neither—and it isn't a choice so much as a balancing act. This is the final chapter of a book that captures part of my teaching story and much of my current knowledge on content-area literacy. The way to point our boat toward growth is to learn the lessons that training and experience provide. Don't make the same mistakes twice is useful advice. If the past is full of mistakes, then remaining firmly focused forward beyond fond reminiscing seems reasonable. I consider it full of stories, which is why this final chapter feels bittersweet; I have enjoyed the nostalgia of learning from mistakes and more.

Live life with few regrets. That seems a better approach; unless one harms others then the regret is best handled with an apology. And forgiveness is our gift. My past was a pasture and I have every reason to believe my future will be too. Not 'put-out-to-pasture' but peaceful and natural, because I can look back with few regrets and look forward with anticipation. I still have chapters ahead. Or chapter, for this book, we are down to the final one. Reflecting on the text makes it clear that teaching literacy is part of every classroom and more. Clear communication is needed for progress and will continue to be, and the biggest question mark of our age is the impact of technology.

I will need to work on my digital skills to keep in touch, because a voice is worth a thousand words only if it is clear and understandable and the online meetings I've attended are often inadequate. One recently echoed and cut out on me twice, so I missed large swatches of the conversation. I also sent out a survey while participating because it was mentioned as a 'need' for progress. I was slightly distracted, but able to listen in as I attached it and wrote a brief note. I hope my keyboard didn't 'clack' and 'click' when I did that. If so, I apologize. I am learning. Still. Always. Technology will constantly be changing so many will feel various levels of with-it-ness. Teachers provide perspective that understands the value in effecting change within the system, if possible. One area where I see the need for change to meet the future is through digital literacies.

This final section only dives into one topic, but it's a doozy:

- Technology

I avoid leadership roles beyond the occasional chairing of committees and the obvious need for controlling a classroom, so that is an area I will not delve into here. I spent one summer working in an office and vowed to never take another administrative or 'leadership' position because it seemed the people in the office spent most of their day dealing with the problems. Putting Band-Aids on boo-boos and working with the disciplinary issues, rules, and regulations. I totally appreciate the administrative-sorts but do not feel passionate enough to write about it. I avoid meetings if possible and have repeatedly said 'no' to requests that I take on positions that take me away from interacting with teachers or future teachers. For those reasons I will not go into leadership issues in this book beyond encouraging us all to be advocates for children and literacy. I recognize my own bias in making this request. Oh, and join organizations and practice action research so you can lead with confidence in the classroom and share with colleagues. There, that is all I want to share about leadership in one paragraph. I recommend an advanced degree if you want to explore literacy leadership in more depth, and I just happen to know a terrific program. Up-sell anyone?

Discussion Questions for Real Writing Practice:

- How do you guide students to use the technology necessary for your field of study?
- In what ways does technology improve learning in your classroom?
- What is the impact of technology in your field?
- What technology do you find most important for guiding learning?

Academics on Technology

The next generation is already here, and the guidance required involves empathy, communication, critical thinking and sisterly love more than any actual direction in how to use technologies. If you're like my family, we tend to hand the gadgets to the young to figure out. Access to the world, through the internet, is at our fingertips and the next generation is always slightly ahead of us in this regard. We can't connect exclusively online, or we risk becoming the cart-riding blobs portrayed in *Walli,* neither can we ignore the impact that technology will continue to have on learning. Research and experience teaches us that learning is too deeply important to not consider the medium and the education of future generations wisely.

Technology is an incredible force in our future and avoiding its siren's song is difficult but the pediatrician's warning of two hours of screen time should be heeded. Technology is valuable for connecting, writing, motivating, data collection, reporting attendance and more but it also takes away from interpersonal interactions and saving paper isn't enough. This is an area that deserves study and focus for our future.

Schools, family and literacy play roles in this process of preparing students to interact in a society increasingly bisected with phones and technology. *Educated* (2017) by Tara Westover provides powerful reasons to question home-schooling and online-exclusive educations. As do reports that many Silicon-Valley executives send their children to schools that ban technology. They know what Turkle (2015) explains in *Reclaiming Conversation.* They know that conversation and talk can be as important as reading and writing. Turkle (2015) shows that too much reliance on devices and social media can be extremely unhealthy, especially for kids. Just like Elvis was extremely unhealthy in the fifties, peace-loving in the sixties, disco and thigh-high boots in the seventies, yuppies in the eighties, gangstas in the nineties, gamers in the turn-of the century and before. Whether that screen be work, play, writing, viewing or a combination, it can't compare to the real world. Awareness of the filter of the screen is part of a healthy relationship with technology.

Question for reflection:

How much technology do we allow in the classroom and why should there be limits? Go. Given what we just learned, don't write, but talk about it. Record your answer to share with class on a device if you are alone.

*****

Real Writing Response:

The 'fun' chapter has me feeling like a cheerleader, but I am not that for technology. I didn't make the cut in seventh-grade. The thickest metal braces with spikes on the back of my bottom teeth were put on the day of try-outs. Four sharp points were placed on my lower teeth to retrain my tongue to rest at the roof of my mouth. It was agony each time I swallowed, which I did over and over in front of the judges. My routine was memorized but darned if I could remember a single move as I stood there, frozen in pain. The scars from that memory are physical and noticeable only if I stick my tongue out at you, which I am unlikely to do. Other scars are invisible. I tried to follow along in time to the music that day, but the pain hindered my performance. That is the agony of defeat, but it didn't slow me down. I attended every game and dance and can be a cheerleader in support for literacy instead.

I would have been a terrible cheerleader with my big-boned clumsiness of middle-school and lack of dance lessons. Not that I asked for lessons in dance. I was too busy building forts in the woods, running with the horses and picking wild strawberries. I did however, ask for tennis lessons. I was twelve and signed up unknowingly for beginner-classes with the five-year-olds to play against. Most were slightly better despite being half my size. I switched over to swim and diving lessons because I could swim like a fish. Generally, we excel where we already have strengths and it makes sense that younger generations, born to a world of advanced technology, excel with portable digital devices. Just like those kids who play tennis at five are more likely to surpass those who start later. I am a decent tennis player as an adult, but that took a blank wall and private lessons. Intense stretching beforehand and a competitive edge won't make me Andre

Agassi but his skill at the sport he hates (2010) demonstrates that success and love are less aligned than success and strengths. I don't have to love technology to understand its significance.

Teaching Critical Digital Literacy (CDL) skills in our schools, as it relates to our content, prepares students to evaluate technology feeds themselves. CDL is the ability to consider the source, context, and truth of information provided digitally. It involves the ability to recognize image manufacturing as an aspect of the digital world. The distinction between digital reality and reality can be determined best when CDL allows everyone to determine what to believe, protecting freedoms while increasing online savvy and safety. Like a firewall for the mind, it provides an awareness of imaging and misrepresentations and offers support for finding the truth in an online world that is constantly changing how we interact with our reality.

Teaching CDL builds to the moment of trust when we believe the weather forecast and climb down into the slot canyon despite fears of flash floods. It is hitting "charge it" and trusting that the selected site will deliver on the promise and that your credit card information is safe. It involves meeting the person you have been communicating with online for the first time, whether in a faraway land or a crowded local coffee shop. It entails casting a vote based, partially, on the online feed that we know is biased, but believe we are capable of interpreting for oneself. Our ability to interact online depends on our level of trust in the systems that protect us. The more positive and honest our interactions the more chance that an online world with integrity can be built and CDL will work. It involves the following elements to start but also requires constant adaptation and evolution because of the rapid changes that occur in the digital world.

Elements of CDL:

1. **Skepticism without cynicism**

If it doesn't feel right it probably isn't for us. But, we can question why we judge too. Would it be fair to judge people because their beliefs differ from ours? There are too many ambiguities to say 'yes' or 'no'. Yes, if their beliefs involve harming others. No if their beliefs do no harm to themselves or others. Again, this can be qualified—we can hurt ourselves for pleasure by eating unhealthy foods or making poor relationship choices or writing painful memories. We can also question these practices and wonder about how then to help drug addicts or prostitutes who may choose another life if circumstances differed. Brutality or building walls, except those to protect us from the truly evil, is not the answer. One complication is that we use digital technologies to communicate and to learn so often. I love the internet and all the conveniences and the fact that I can check out at the grocery store without ever interacting with another human. I wear earbuds and love that Facebook is customizable so that the news I see most often is from family and friends and involves pictures of baby animals and Southwestern conferences and yoga exercises and books and teaching. I also understand that this means anyone watching, and the advertisers are clearly watching, knows quite a bit about me. I am open and available on digital technologies, but I am also aware of the skewed view of the world I see online, and I am aware that the image and the reality are often not truly aligned. Teaching how to recognize and find the truth online is a complex skill that involves questioning and probing while remaining open-minded. The exact questions can't be known beforehand, but an inquiring mind can be developed and nurtured so that the exponential growth of information available can be handled by literate digital citizens.

An example of skepticism without cynicism: "Time is my fortune and I choose to spend it on you." How this sounds depends on who we are and the circumstances of our world. If this is Mother Theresa speaking to God, then I can accept that she was a good person doing what she truly believed was the best she could to live a devoted life. As a cynic I can wonder if teaching others to accept their "lot" in life is truly God's work or if it is a control mechanism for the masses. As a skeptic I accept her devotion and love of the poor and, while still questioning the structure of our society and the role that religion plays, I accept that her choices did no intentional harm.

2. Prioritization

Is this Mother Theresa speaking to God? A mother to her son? A lover? A man to his business? If basic needs are met, then time really is the only fortune we spend. How we spend it depends on the extent to which we control our own time. Meeting basic needs can be consuming and not leave time to process and consider priorities. To do this we must understand our own individual values. What earns space in your head and your life? One skill worthy of teaching is how to keep your digital feed focused on what matters. My husband's stories often end with death, as in "a guy went whitewater rafting in a crocodile-infested river after being warned by natives that they don't even wash their clothing or gather drinking water from the banks without a club in hand. Can we guess what happened to him? Well, the last he was seen he was in the jaws of a two-hundred-pound crocodile. Want to see the picture?" This part of our digital reality can be used for personal safety. It is a priority for him, so this is a reasonable approach if fear doesn't rule. I am confident that I won't be in the jungle kayaking anytime soon so I don't feel I need that warning. I do want to know if the roads are icy though. I can decide how to make my online presence and feed match my priorities. This decision is one way I control the impact of digital technologies and it is a skill worthy of teaching and considering in our digital worlds.

Prioritization is complicated because what we value changes as we mature and gain wisdom and because we must understand our own and accept others. Accepting others doesn't translate immediately into spending our time on them though. Balancing what deserves our time and attention with all the distractions deserves to be taught explicitly. Labels, such as "productive worker" can be tied to the ability to monitor email and respond insightfully. Awareness deserves to be called to the difference between this and the 'look at me, working hard' at odd-hours email. Finding balance was already difficult when 'work' automatically meant leaving home. The need to recognize the relationship between how we spend our time and our priorities is about finding alignment amongst our many roles, both personal and public.

3. Keep it real

This isn't some kind of 'feel good' step. This isn't about letting go of fears and stress and realizing that all we can do is focus on the small positives and wonders of each day to fortify for battling the dark side. Nor is it about winning each successive battle by being positive and selecting the soundtrack and the feed of your life. Writing your own story. All that is up to you, and your path is your choice – but can we at least agree to be honest?

A level of honesty is necessary for sanity and progress in our digital futures. Fact checking is a learned skill and naïve trust is not suggested so teachers guide students to make sound choices. Real-world experiences are needed. The Grand Canyon cannot be known without standing on its edge. An image mass produced to sell to the voters cannot be understood through only a digital medium. So far, the proxy versions have worked. If our government begins to fail us, then more questions and skepticism and prioritizations will be imperative. Learning to recognize mistruths doesn't mean focusing on the critical aspects of the world. Beauty matters. By using CDL we can increase the chance that attempts to help the misfortunate of the world have a positive impact. We increase the chance that those who need kindness and fair treatments get their needs met. That is beautiful. Or, if we vote based on ads or headlines or news feed, using CDL we check our sources and have conversations with intelligent people of diverse views. Remaining honest and open-minded is important even when the lessons are hard. Sometimes, especially when they are hard.

4. Limit exposure

Time is a component of CDL that is more complicated than expected. We need time in all kinds of situations and digital realities can isolate us even as we connect online. The exploration and the sense of wonder at having the world at your fingertips can be addictive. Yet, our sun must shine from up in the sky not the manufactured rays of a screen or bulb. Stop talking and writing and listen to the birds and nature and the people around us. Break and breathe the fresh air. I don't have to leave my house to work. I don't have to interact with anyone to go to the bank or store or gas station. These are positive because I save my interactions for family, work colleagues, students or friends. Thus, this is related to the teaching of prioritization. Limiting exposure means prioritizing interactions offline. Conversing with real people helps us to improve our communication skills and learn. Finding balance in this area helps us to grow and improve as people and that is how we move forward and meet the future. Evolution of our race didn't stop just because we no longer need to outrun the jaguars; exercise matters. CDL can be utilized as a tool for monitoring time so we maintain a healthy relationship with the world around us.

I continue to see examples of the internet policing itself and I am heartened. A website I used as an example of the need for CDL in the past (www.martinlutherking.org) now takes you to a page that says "Sorry" and asks you to click a link if you are the owner of that page. I believe the owner was most-likely KKK-affiliated, so I am pleased to see it shut down. For years it came up in the first page of search results if you Googled Martin Luther King. It was awful, and it was a perfect example of why it is important to teach future generations to utilize technology with an awareness of the need for caution.

Learning Moment:

Time heals. I started this book at a time when I thought to share it with my mother, mostly. She would have enjoyed a literacy book where she knows the people involved and as a reading teacher she would have shared her feedback. Instead, I share it with all of you. We are all our brother's keeper and learning, as always, leads us into the future. Let's go arm-in-arm, shall we?

Thank you for reading. Namaste.

Appendices:

Entry #1: The conceptual models used by my college.

Teacher-as-Decision-Maker Model

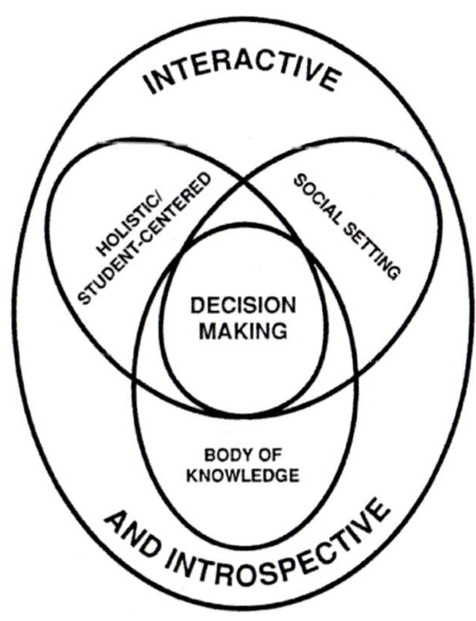

This creation was well-researched, and no one disagreed with the tenets, but it was replaced with this:

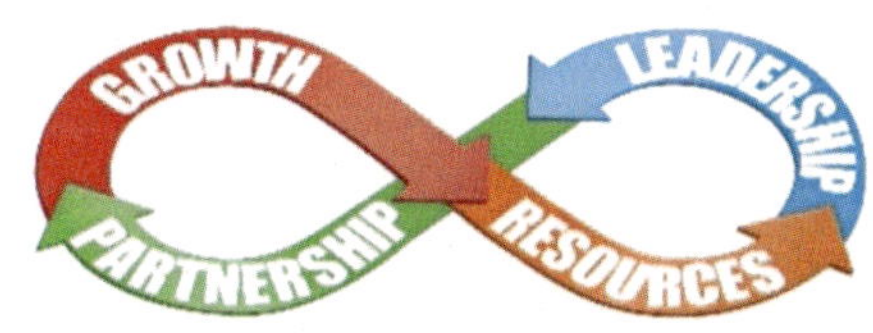

The emphasis on teachers who are provided the resources for growth with supportive leadership makes sense. The leadership comes from each teacher autonomously and from administration. A partnership is built on trust with the community served. The infinity loop recognizes the cyclical nature of learning and growing for both teachers and students. The need for calm waters and guidance along with figuring out the deep end is represented with the flowing nature of the infinity loop.

Entry #2: Lesson Plan Format

Each teacher writes their own plans based on more factors than need recorded for each lesson. That said, here is a guide to strategies and lesson planning that can assist in the process:

Components for Planning Units and Daily Agendas:

1. Standards/Engagement/Goals: What is the content and why is it relevant and worthy of priority?
2. Assessment/Measurements/Skills: When will I know that students understand and can build on this concept or move on?
3. Guided Practice/Strategies/Methods: How will I impart the content and skills to students so that it becomes part of their schema? How do I match instruction with my strengths as a teacher and my students' learning styles?
4. Literacy/Critical Thinking/ Extensions. Have I included communication skills that students will need to succeed in becoming independent thinkers in my content area? Have I challenged students to think critically?

- Marzano high yield methods of teaching (2012)
    - Identifying similarities and differences
    - Summarizing and note taking
    - Reinforcing effort and providing recognition
    - Homework and practice
    - Non-linguistic representations
    - Cooperative learning
    - Setting objectives and providing feedback
    - Generating and testing hypotheses
    - Cue, questions, and advanced organizers

5. Guidance/Differentiation/Diversity/Interventions: How will I start and end lessons to build continuity and connect what is learned with other academic subjects and these students? How will I use assessment results to guide student learning? How will I intervene for those who struggle?
6. Reflection/Analysis: The practice of writing/thinking about the classroom to learn from both positive and negative experiences and data to improve instruction. What went well? What should improve?

GO DEEP: Guidelines for reflecting:

G: Guide your thinking beyond the "I had a good day" or "my timing was off" level by analyzing and reflecting as often as possible and sometimes by giving yourself time in class to think/write notes too. Teachers are decision makers and making informed decisions is enhanced by reflection. Don't skip this valuable step.

O: Observe: try to imagine that you are a researcher recording the specific details to determine what can be learned from close examination.

D: Diverse Perspectives: Talk and listen to those around you to solicit perspectives that can enhance your reflections and improve your classroom. Reflecting in a vacuum is less valuable than reflection that considers and solicits others' views. Students, colleagues, parents, administration—you are part of a community that is focused on student success so discuss it and learn together.

E: Experiment—try different approaches to reflecting. Maybe you scribble notes on plans or maybe you script out what to say next time. There isn't a wrong way to reflect if it leads to progress.

E: Explore—Consider both the positives and negative experiences and realize that you can build upon your strengths and improve in needed areas only if you recognize both.

P: Prioritize—focus your reflections on what is truly important in the classroom—learning and the interactions that lead there.

Entry #3: A **Concept Ladder** (Allen, 2007) is another option for exploring the specific concept of graphic organizers.

Concept:
Graphic Organizers

Language associated with it:

- Visualization
- Charts and Graphs

Reasons to use it:
Because the visual representation of the information provides students with a tool for considering the new material in a different way.

Kinds of Graphic Organizers:

- Venn Diagram
- Frayer Model
- Webs/Concept Maps
- Double-entry Diary (Tovani)
- Etcetera… too many to list.

Questions regarding it:
What is the content being taught and how might it be enhanced by visual representation?

Can the students design their own visual and would that be worth the time?

Does this relate to note-taking and could I teach my students to take notes in a visually appealing manner by modeling note-taking and talking through the process used to capture the concept?

Connection to teaching:
Just taking content and putting it into boxes does not necessarily make an organizer effective. To make this strategy work my questions need to build upon each other so that the steps make sense. We go from basic knowledge-level to the schematics of the brain and learning and this box takes us back to the main lesson of this section: design your own graphic organizers that are aligned with the learning objectives. Use your autonomy to make it great.

Glossary of terms:

Education from A to Z: A Dictionary of terms for Education

These terms were gathered with input from the TEMS faculty: Drs. Patricia Calahan (PC), Jonathon Gould (JG), and Rodney Williams (RW) under the auspices of Dr. Anne Tapp (AT) in her role as director of clinical experiences. She emphasized the importance of knowing the current lingo in a world of ever-changing jargon. Where you see their initials below is the main part of their contribution area.

Introduction

This dictionary is not meant to be comprehensive for your specific field of study and cannot contain all the possible acronyms of Special Education or the many other fields that impact educators. But, these are the terms and concepts worthy of time and attention in this text. This dictionary includes the terms of importance for Real Writing. How we organize the information so that the brain remembers is important for learning.

Category:	Definition	Relation to Real Writing
Assessment	A process of gathering data to measure what a student knows and understands as a result of instruction.	Writing is a great tool for assessing literacy skills in any subject and literacy levels play a role in results.
Classroom Climate	The environment for learning that a teacher and students create.	We all learn best in a supportive environment and the "Real" part of real writing is about building relationships that enhance learning.
Delivery of Instruction	How one presents materials to learners.	Real writing is used in the planning and the execution of most lessons.
Differentiation	How one individualizes so students' specific learning needs are met.	The key components of literacy (speaking, listening, writing, and reading) are all options for modes of differentiation and making it real for the student results in lessons that teach content to a variety of students.
Equity	Fair; impartial; Just.	Notice that the definition isn't 'equal'. Equity is about using a fair process for teaching and real writing is one option.
Learner Development	The concept that learning happens in stages, with guidance and time.	This is the goal of schooling and clearly relates to the choices we make for content and pedagogy.
Literacy	Competence or knowledge in a certain area.	The definition is broad, but literacy is an overarching concept that is developed in any subject area along with cooperation, numeracy, and skills. Once basic proficiency is attained then the learning can become more complex.
Technology	All the possible screens in the classroom, unless you consider window screens, or you have a room divider.	Writing done on a screen seems more real to the next generation because it is easily 'out there' but moderation of screen-time is recommended in the interest of keeping it real.

You'll notice repetition in the chart above. The connection to real writing is established firmly using that repetition. I try not to repeat myself but find it a useful tool at times.

This section of the text isn't meant to be read from start to finish like the rest. It is a resource to refer to as the concepts are discussed in other chapters. Some of the vocabulary words here are not mentioned elsewhere. The decisions about what to include and what not to include was a collaborative effort with my colleagues. The group approved all the entries and thus a compromise was struck.

Assessment

Key Terms:

- **Affective Assessment:** An assessment that measures a medley of non-cognitive variables such as a person's attitudes, interests, and values. (JG)
- **Authentic assessment:** An attempt to replicate real-world measurements of knowledge and understanding in an academic setting.
- **Diagnostic Assessment:** Also known as pre-assessment; this measures students' prior knowledge, strengths, and areas of need so that instruction can be tailored to the individual.
- **Feedback:** Input used to guide learning that can involve identifying strengths and areas of need
- **Formative assessment:** This is assessment that occurs during the learning process to modify instruction if necessary so that learning is optimized. (RW; DS)
- **Reliability**: This is an assessment term that refers to data being consistent over multiple measurements. So, if we want to know how well students support their argument we measure this not just on a test, but also with a debate and maybe as a homework assignment too. This is why we vary our assessment tools – so that

students have multiple ways to demonstrate their learning and we have reliable data.

- **Rigor:** The challenge involved in an assignment or activity. Rigor is impacted by teacher expectations, the level of the materials and the level of the questions asked.
- **Rubric:** A tool used to standardize grading and set expectations/criteria for an assignment.
- **Standardized test:** A test of skills or knowledge that has undergone measures to objectify the grading so that comparisons can be made with a level of reliability and validity.
- **Summative Assessment:** This is assessment that occurs after the instruction process to measure students' knowledge or skills.
- **Validity:** This is an assessment term that refers to data being accurate, based on the measurement aligning with what is supposed to be measured. So, if I want to test my students' knowledge of grammar and I give them a multiple-choice exam the results may be less valid than if I assign a paragraph of writing and check it for grammar mistakes. If our assessment tool is aligned with content and standards, then it will provide more valid data.

***Current Jargon/Policies to Know (AT):*

- **Every Student Succeeds Act** (ESSA): The Every Student Succeeds ACT (ESSA) was signed by President Obama in 2015. It reauthorized the 50-year-old Elementary and Secondary Education Act (ESEA) (PC)
- **Highly Qualified Teachers (HQT)**: The term used to describe teachers who are teaching in their area of expertise/certification.
- **Michigan Revised School Code:** Does your state have one too? (ACT 451 of 1976) The act that provides for a system of public instruction in Michigan. This code regulates certification of teachers, evaluation systems for schools and teachers and election of school board, funding of schools, etc.
- **No Child Left Behind (NCLB):** This law scaled up the federal role in holding schools accountable for student outcomes. It has been replaced with the ESSA.

- **Northwest Evaluation Association** (NWEA)**:** An online evaluation system aligned with content standards and designed to measure growth and skills.

- **Smarter Balanced Assessment Consortium** (SBAC): An online assessment system based out of the University of California that is aligned with common core state standards.

Classroom Climate

Key Terms:

- **Bullying**: Forcing others to do what you want by superior strength, power, or intimidation tactics. Both bullies and those who are bullied are often victims among children and those with low self-esteem are often prone to bullying.
- **Classroom Management**: One's system of establishing an environment for learning. This is impacted by who we are and who we are teaching.
- **Disposition:** One's temperament and qualities that impact classroom behavior and performance.
- **Engagement:** The amount to which the students are paying attention enough to be learning. This occurs when students are challenged, supported, and interested in learning enough to think about your subject and relate it to their education and lives.
- **Legitimacy:** Acceptance of authority that occurs when the subjects have a voice and feel the rules are consistent and fair.
- **Motivation (extrinsic and intrinsic):** The reason one has for behaving or responding in a certain way. Intrinsic motivation is doing an activity for enjoyment while extrinsic motivation involves doing an activity for an external reward or to avoid punishment.
- **Resistance Theory:** Proposes that students actively or passively resist learning as a way of responding to the oppressive school system. "Resistance theories demonstrate how individuals

negotiate and struggle with structures and create meanings of their own from these interactions." (Bernal & Solorzano, 2001, p. 315).

- **Teacher Expectations:** A complicated relationship exists between these and student achievement. These are often influenced by students' behaviors and the teachers' own biases.
- **Mindset:** An individual's beliefs or way of thinking. Those with a *fixed* mindset believe that ability is mostly innate and failure results from a lack of the necessary basic abilities. Those with a *growth* mindset believe they can acquire any ability provided they invest effort or study. (PC; DS)
- **Victimology:** The study of learned helplessness and other impacts of being a victim and the ways to intervene or overcome psychological effects.
- **With-it-ness:** Being aware of the classroom and knowing how to respond to situations that arise.

***Current Jargon to Know (AT):*

- **Real Talk:** Instructor led discussions focused on a series of broad engaging themes which are created and shared to establish connections, build rapport, and gain insight into students' perceptions of the world. (Hernandez, 2015).

Delivery of Instruction

Key Terms:

- **Backward Design:** Designing curriculum in three stages: 1.) Setting goals/aligning with standards; 2.) Planning instruction; 3.) Assessing in order to set revised goals. This is a cyclical structure for curriculum planning.
- **Bloom's Taxonomy:** a hierarchical model of thinking that builds from basics such as remembering, comprehending, applying to

more critical forms of thinking such as analyzing, synthesizing, and evaluating (PC; DS)

- **Closure:** This is a component for the end of a lesson and the end of class. Closure of a lesson involves leaving in such a way that a lasting impression is formed. Closure of a class involves reminding students of the learning that may have occurred and building anticipation for the next class.
- **Content Standards:** Learning goals for each content area that outline what a student should know and be able to do at the end of each grade. Each content area has national standards that relate to your own discipline in addition to any state standards or content expectations.
- **Cooperative Learning:** A method of teaching that requires students to cooperate with each other to learn. This works best when modeled, structured to include mixed ability groupings and structured so that each student plays a role in the accomplishment of a common task.
- **Depth of Knowledge**: a model of labeling critical thinking related to rigor in education. The stages are: I. Recall/Reproduction; II. Skill/Concept; III. Strategic Thinking; and IV. Extended Thinking (PC; DS)
- **Guided Practice/During:** The delivery of instruction phase associated with helping students to understand the concepts and skills as it is presented.
- **Hook/Into:** The start of a lesson that is intended to catch the learner's interest by building relevancy and curiosity.
- **Lesson Planning:** Planning for the daily business of teaching that can include all components, or a mixture based on students' needs and the goals for the class.
- **Metacognition:** Thinking about your own thinking processes.
- **Relevancy:** How much a lesson relates to students' actual lives…outside their school lives, so grades don't count. Except we know that they do count, and wanting to please the teacher, and knowing how to please the teacher, and so many other complicating factors. But, we strive towards authenticity. The more relevant the better the educational experience.

- **Schema:** The wiring of our brain and the understanding that we all come to the classroom with a different set of experiences and backgrounds that influence learning.
- **Standards:** The content and the behaviors and the academic expectations that we prioritize in our classrooms.
- **Strategy:** An instructional strategy is a tool used to increase achievement in the classroom. Strategies should be based on research. Your methods (or approach) can include strategies but is a more general term that refers to your procedures for running your lesson. So, for example, you can use cooperative learning methods to have students complete a Venn Diagram (strategy).
- **Wait time:** The amount of time we provide for students to answer a question. If wait time is consistently adequate in the classroom it sends a message that you value students' thinking and participation. (DS; PC)
- **Zone of Proximal Development** (ZPD): "The distance between the actual developmental level as determined by independent problem solving and the level of potential development as determined through problem solving under adult guidance, or in collaboration with more capable peers". (Vygotsky, 1978, p. 86). (PC; DS)

***Current Jargon/Policies to Know (AT):*

- **Common Core State Standards** (CCSS)/College Ready standards: "a set of high-quality academic standards in mathematics and English language arts/literacy (ELA). These learning goals outline what a student should know and be able to do at the end of each grade." These standards were adopted in 2010 in Michigan.
- **Flipped Classroom:** When you do things in reverse, such as give guided work time during class and assign reading at home or make/show videos to provide content and then use class-time to discuss, reflect and learn about the content so that guidance can be provided based on learners' needs and interests.

- **Michigan Merit Curriculum (MMC):** The requirements for high school graduation in the state of Michigan. All students who earn a diploma, at a minimum, have demonstrated proficiency with the content outlined by the state academic standards or guidelines.

- **Professional Learning Community** (PLC): A group of educators who meet periodically, over an extended period, to enhance their competencies related to one or more topics. (PC)
- **Project Based Learning:** An approach in which students gain knowledge and skills by working for an extended time to investigate and respond to an engaging and complex question, problem, or challenge.
- **STEM**: Science, Technology, Engineering and Mathematics, sometimes referred to as STEAM with the addition of Arts.

Differentiation

Key Terms:

- **Attention Deficit/Hyperactivity Disorder** (ADHD/ADD): A developmental disorder resulting in limited attention span and impulse control issues; a medical diagnosis is required.
- **Bilingual Education:** Teaching academic content in two languages so the primary language and secondary language are both developed and utilized for learning.
- **Cognitive Impairment:** An impairment of the brain that results in learning difficulties.
- **English Language Learner (ELL):** A person who is learning English in addition to their primary language. Related terms include *English as a Second Language (ESL), Teaching English to Speakers of Other Languages (TESOL) and Limited English Proficiency (LEP).*
- **Inclusion:** Placing students with disabilities alongside their non-disabled peers to learn.

- **Individual Education Program** (IEP): A program of study created by a team focused upon meeting the needs of an individual special education student. This document is reviewed and updated yearly.
- **Emotional Impairment (EI):** An inability to form connections with teachers and peers that results in learning difficulties.
- **Giftedness:** High intellectual ability. Gifted and talented programs are intended to provide optimal learning situations for gifted students to develop.
- **Intervention:** A remediation attempt for students who are identified as struggling academically or behaviorally.
- **Learning Styles:** The concept that there are multiple ways of learning and that every person learns differently.

***Current Jargon/Policies to Know (AT):*

- **504 plan:** A plan to ensure that a student who has a disability identified under the law receives accommodations to ensure their academic success and access to the learning environment.
- **Family Educational Rights and Privacy Act (FERPA):** Protects the privacy of students' educational records.
- **Individuals with Disabilities Education Act:** (IDEA) Federal legislation spelling out educational services for those with disabilities.(PC)
- **Multi-Tiered System of Support (MTSS):** An umbrella term that encompasses RTI and PBIS.
- **Positive Behavioral Interventions and Support (PBIS):** A tiered system that identifies students with behavioral issues at school and intervenes systemically based on the needs of the students.
- **Response to Intervention (RTI):** A multi-tiered intervention program used to provide early, systematic, and appropriately intensive assistance to students who are at-risk for underperforming academically.
- **Universal Design for Learning** (UDL): A framework that addresses one barrier to learning within instructional

environments: inflexible, “one-size-fits-all” curricula. UDL offers guidelines to create flexible learning environments designed to accommodate all learners. (DS; PC)

Equity

Key Terms:

- **Assimilation:** How people change to become part of a group culture.
- **Cultural Competence**: Having an awareness of one’s cultural identity and views about difference, and the ability to learn and build on the varying cultural and community norms of students and their families.
- **Cultural Capital:** The cultural knowledge that serves as currency and helps us to navigate culture and alters our experiences and the opportunities available to us.
- **Culturally Responsive Teaching:** An approach to teaching that values and understands students’ cultural heritage and histories and brings high expectations and positive perceptions of students and their families into the classroom.
- **Culture Shock:** The disorientation felt when one experiences a culture very different than one’s own.
- **Discrimination:** Unjust treatment of people based on intolerance for differences.
- **Ethnocentrism:** Judging others’ cultures with preconceptions based on one’s own customs and ways of life.
- **Gender:** Behaviors that result from the social, cultural, and psychological factors associated with masculinity and femininity in society. Male and female roles result from the socialization of the individual within a group.
- **Marginalization:** Treatment of a group, person, or concept as insignificant or peripheral.

- **Multicultural Education (ME):** A total school reform effort designed to increase educational equity for a range of cultural, ethnic, and economic groups. The four dimensions of ME are content integration, knowledge construction process, prejudice reduction, and equity pedagogy.
- **Nonsexist Education:** An approach to education that does not discriminate based on gender stereotypes.
- **Resiliency Theory:** The understanding that the presence of one or more protective factors can reduce the effects of exposure to adversity.
- **Poverty:** A state of living in substandard conditions due to extreme poorness. Poverty often drastically disadvantages students in the school setting.
- **Prejudice:** Judging someone inferior based on stereotypes or expectations rather than actual interactions or experiences.
- **Race:** An attempt by physical anthropologists to divide human groups according to their physical traits and characteristics. This has proven to be difficult because groups in modern societies are highly mixed physically. Consequently, different and often conflicting race typologies exist.
- **Self-Awareness:** An understanding that our backgrounds and experiences impact our expectations and attitudes regarding those who are different than us and the realization that even progressive thinkers harbor unconscious biases.
- **Sexual Orientation:** How a human identifies in terms of gender and attraction.
- **Social Class/Socio-Economic Status (SES):** The stratification of humans into a status hierarchy based on wealth that is often linked with power. Also, a collection of people who have similar economic status based on such criteria as income, occupation, education, values, behaviors, and life chances. Lower, working, middle, and upper are common designators in the US.

- **Tracking:** Ability grouping in academic settings. There is "a virtual mountain of research evidence indicating that homogeneous grouping doesn't consistently help anyone learn better" (Oakes, 1985, p. 7).
- **White Privilege:** The unearned advantages or benefits of being white.

***Current Jargon/Policies to Know (AT):*

- Current categories for sexual identification include lesbian, gay, bisexual, transgender, queer, questioning, intersex, and asexual.
- **Heteronormativity:** A set of lifestyle norms, practices, and institutions that promote binary alignment of biological sex, gender identity, and gender roles; assume heterosexuality as a fundamental and natural norm; and privilege monogamous, committed relationships and reproductive sex above all other sexual practices.
- **MI Code of Ethics:** Does your state have one? The following ethical standards are included for all professional educators in the state of Michigan: 1.) service toward the common good; 2.) mutual respect; 3.) equity; 4.) diversity; and 5.) truth and honesty.
- **Preferred Gender Pronoun (PGP):** The set of pronouns that an individual would like others to use when talking to or about that individual.

Learner Development

Key Terms:

- **Developmentally Appropriate Practices:** Providing an environment and offering content, strategies, and approaches that are aligned with students' levels of readiness.

- **Formal Operations Stage:** This stage begins at around the age of twelve and lasts into adulthood; it is characterized by the ability to understand abstract thoughts and reason logically.
- **Generalization:** The tendency to respond the same way to different but similar stimuli. The use of past learning for current situations.
- **Imaginary Audience:** The egocentric belief often associated with adolescents, that one is the center of attention for others.
- **Learned Helplessness:** If humans or other animals have been abused and unable to escape they learn that trying to escape is hopeless. Therefore, they don't try to get out of bad situations in the future. They accept the loss of control and give up trying. (PC)
- **Learned Strength:** If humans get positive feedback and support they learn that hope springs eternal. So, be that positive in the life of a student. Make school a safe and supportive environment so that we can foster a sense of independence and strength among the marginalized of the world.
- **Levels of Moral Development:** A theory to explain how humans advance from following rules for fear of punishment through stages toward a justice orientation. According to Kohlberg, social experiences can promote our moral development by stimulating our mental processes. As we discuss and debate hypothetical situations and find our views challenged, our thinking must reflect broader viewpoints (Kohlberg et al., 1975).
- **Sense of Belonging:** A basic human need for community that is established when one feels accepted as a member of the group.
- **Social Identity Theory:** Whenever groups are identified and labeled members of in-groups favor in-group members and discriminate against out-group members.
- **Stereotype Threat:** The risk of confirming negative stereotypes about an individual's cultural, ethnic, gender, or racial group.

***Current Jargon/Policies to Know (AT):*

- This was not an area as influenced by current jargon as others. Any suggestions?

Literacy

Key Terms:

- **Critical Literacy:** An approach to literacy that values questioning the sources, purposes, and context of a text. This approach purposefully exposes misrepresentations or under-representations of certain groups in the texts used for learning.
- **Dyslexia:** A reading disorder based on difficulty relating speech sounds to letters and words.
- **Frye's Graph:** A tool used to find the grade-level of written text that relies on sentence length and word length to determine difficulty.
- **Proficient Reader Research:** Research into the cognitive strategies that proficient readers automatically use for comprehension. These include visualization, inquiry, predicting, and connecting along with monitoring their own progress and inferring the main ideas. This has been shown to be effective when taught explicitly for content area learning from texts and other sources.
- **Stages of a Lesson:** Three stages are encouraged to teach literacy skills. 1.) Into or schema activation is used to establish a purpose, activate background knowledge and sustain motivation. 2.) Through or interaction stage guides students to prompt an active response to texts. 3.) The beyond stage extends and elaborates upon ideas from the text.
- **Triadic Model:** A model to represent the interaction between the reader, the context, and the text that occurs to create meaning from texts. This relates closely to the Michigan Definition of Reading which links "the reader's existing knowledge, the meaning suggested by the writer's language, and the context of the reading situation" for teaching comprehension.

***Current Jargon/Policies to Know (AT):*

- **Digital Literacy:** "The ability to use information and communication technologies to find, evaluate, create, and communicate information, requiring both cognitive and technical skills" (ILA).
- **Disciplinary Literacy:** The confluence of content knowledge, experiences, and skills merged with the ability to read, write, listen, speak, think critically and perform in a way that is meaningful within the context of a given field.
- **International Literacy Association (ILA):** The organization that sets most literacy standards for the US.

Technology

Key Terms:

- **Assistive Technology:** Devices and programs designed to help those with disabilities.
- **Learner Management Systems (LMS):** A software application for the delivery of educational courses or training programs.
- **Technology Standards:** In 2008 the International Society for Technology in Education (ISTE) issued its National Educational Technology Standards for Teachers (NETS-T) which include standards relating to learning and creativity, assessment, digital citizenship, and professional growth and leadership.

***Current Jargon to Know (AT):*

- **Kahoot!: A** game-based learning platform for quizzing students in the classroom.
- **Netiquette:** Manners for online communications.

- **Prezi:** Zooming presentation software that uses motion and spatial relationships.
- **Skyward:** A software package used in schools to manage and store information and network with parents and families.

Ten final lessons:

1. Don't rush your lessons and expect to relearn some with each new situation and class. This is natural progression and should not be accompanied by a face-palm unless you really did goof. Take notes to increase your chances of avoiding the same pitfalls.

2. The lessons are always changing and thus will mean different things with multiple readings. So, I suggest revisiting the learning moments and answering these questions:

- How does this lesson relate to me (**real writing moment**)?
- What question do I still have regarding this content?
- How does this relate to the content I teach?
- What 'academics' support the answer I found to the question?

This is the process, not always linear, in reverse, used to write this text. By relating each of the lessons to your situation and questions, you can grow in knowledge and then implement and reflect.

3. Allow yourself the space to reflect without censure. Space. It isn't something we often consider in teaching, but it is important. One way to find space is learning to say "no". There are so many forces competing for our time and attention that the focus on student achievement sometimes gets overlooked. Don't let it by learning to say 'no' to meetings that you do not find linked while remaining professional and courteous. This one

may have fit in the 'leadership' section. Or, I can refer to my article. Does anyone read those articles?

4. Work toward balance. Challenge but don't make the work so difficult that revolt is necessary. Nice but not lax and professional without becoming distant. Find your own style and embrace it while remaining willing to grow and improve in all areas. Avoid rigmarole, if possible.

5. Improve communications.

6. Hunger for the truth in the classroom and motivate students by connecting to universal themes. We all have our version of truth for these concepts. Think HOME, FAMILY, LOVE, JUSTICE, DEATH, NUMBERS, etc. This creates a background knowledge link.

7. Laughter in the classroom and in the discussions surrounding it is valuable if it is kind. Use sarcasm with the greatest care and avoid humiliation unless of the kind that one laughs off immediately. This is the spaghetti-in-the-air moment that means we don't laugh before Plugsie is deemed safe and sound. Build trust and caring and then laughter can follow.

8. Remember to breathe too. Take in the fresh air. Countdown for excitement and let the pressure be positive towards creativity and progress and mindful of the need for restorative breaks (June, July, or a Friday night) to be our best selves.

9. Don't Cheat. I have a legitimate reason to believe that cheating is a poor choice. My mother cheated on her eye exam as a child. She was following her sister and listened and memorized the letters and repeated them back

to the doctor. If she hadn't done this she would have benefitted from a patch over her working eye and would have gained peripheral vision. My mother died in a car accident caused by her lack of peripheral vision. She also suffered from neck pain throughout her adult life that she attributed to the tilt of her head caused by the need to adjust her vision to make up for one lazy eye. This is a real reason not to cheat. Of course, some areas of cheating are less important. I climbed back into the window of my Geography class during senior year and completed tests on the countries of the world with no ill effect. I can navigate and read a map if I need to and in New York City I have found the locals helpful and polite when I ask directions. I will never need to know all the countries of the World. That is what Google is for and if I can't look it up then I am probably playing a game like Trivial Pursuit. Losing at a game does not matter.

10. Question without interrogating. Listen and consider before interjecting. Sometimes it is difficult to translate, but if you truly listen then you will understand. We are swinging on a pendulum of time. For this book it is almost out. What questions remain for you?

Slightly Annotated Works Cited

Please keep reading; the sources for the ideas deserve to be part of the book rather than footnotes. This section is often ignored unless one is a researcher or finds a reference particularly interesting. I love Stephen King's list of 'must read' books at the end of *On Writing* almost as much as the rest of his book. Alas, I am no Stephen King, with ten thousand hours of horror under my belt, but I do have more than that invested in teaching literacy and reading about it from these sources and more.

Abeles, V. (2015). *Beyond measure: Rescuing an overscheduled, overtested, understimulated generation.* New York, NY: Simon and Schuster.

Agassi, A. (2010). *Open.* New York, NY: Vintage books.

Allen, J. (2007). *Inside Words: Tools for teaching academic vocabulary grades 4-12.* Portland, MA: Stenhouse Publishers.

Al Samawi, M. (2018). *Fox hunt: A refugee's memoir of coming to America.* New York, NY: Harper Collins.

Anyon, J. (1980). Social Class and the hidden curriculum of work. *Journal of Education.* 162 (1): 67-92.

Asher, J. (1969). The Total Physical Response approach to second language learning. *The Modern Language Journal.* 53 (1): 3-17.

Bambrick-Santoya, P. (2010). *Driven by data: A practical guide to improve instruction.* San Francisco, CA: Jossey-Bass.

Banks, J.A. & Banks, C.A. (2001). *Multicultural education: Issues and perspectives.* New York, NY: John Wiley & Sons.

Chickering, A.W. & Gamson, Z.F. (1987) Seven principles for good practice in undergraduate education. *American Association of Higher Education Bulletin.* 39 (7):3-7.

Chambliss, W.J. (2003). Saints and the Roughnecks. In Hancock, B.W. & Sharp, P.M. (Eds.), *Criminal Justice in America: Theory, Practice, and Policy*. (pp. 343-355). London, UK: Pearson.

Daniels, H. & Zemelman, S. (2014). *Subjects matter: Exceeding Standards through Powerful Content-Area Reading* (second edition). Portsmouth, NH: Heinemann. This is the book I recommend on my syllabus. These authors have been my gurus providing instruction and inspiration from afar for years.

Daniels, H. (2002). *Literature Circles: Voice and choice in book clubs and reading groups*. Markham, Ontario: Pembroke Publishers.

Delpit, L. (2002). The skin that we speak: Thoughts on language and culture in the classroom. New York, NY: The New Press.

Delpit, L. (1995/2006) Other People's Children: Cultural Conflict in the Classroom. New York, NY. The New Press. Delpit made issues regarding race and class of interest to me and guided my learning about my own language and skin with both of her books.

Freire, P. (1972). *Pedagogy of the oppressed.* New York, NY: Herder and Herder.

Gardner, H. (2006). *Multiple Intelligences.* New York, NY: Basic Books.

Gladwell, M. (2008). *Outliers: The Story of Success*. Boston, MA: Little Brown and Company. Brilliant. This is the book I would currently say each teacher should read and understand. Gladwell explains how the exceptions to the rule follow another set of rules to be exceptional.

Gladwell, M. (2015). *David and Goliath: Underdogs, Misfits, and the Art of Battling Giants.* Boston, MA: Little Brown and Company.

Grant, A. (2016). *Originals: How nonconformists move the world.* New York; NY; Penguin Books.

Grant, C.A. & Gillette. (2006). A candid talk to teacher educators about effectively preparing teachers who can teach everyone's children. *Journal of Teacher Education.* 57(3): 292-299.

Heath, S.B. (1983). *Ways with words: Language, life and work in communities and classrooms*. Cambridge, England: Cambridge University Press.

Hendrix, H. (2008). *Getting the love you want: A guide for couples.* New York, NY: Saint Martin's Press.

Hernandez, P. (2015) *The Pedagogy of Real Talk.* Thousand Oaks, CA: Sage/Corwin. This one deserves stars, based on how much I use it. If you ever get to see Paul talk in person, I highly recommend it. He is an awesome leader of teachers.

Hutchinson, J.N. (1999). *Students on the margins: Education, stories, dignity*. Albany, NY: State University of New York Press.

Kagan, S. (2013). *Kagan cooperative learning structures.* San Clemente, CA: Kagan Publishing.

King, S. (2010). *On writing: A memoir of the craft.* New York, NY: Scribner.

Kohl, H. (2005). *She Would Not Be Moved.* New York: The New Press. pp. 7-8.

Kohlberg, L. (1985). The just community approach to moral education in theory and practice. In Berkowitz, M.W. & Oser, F. (Eds.), *Moral education: Theory and application.* (pp. 27-88). Hillsdale, NJ: Lawrence Erlbaum Associates.

Kohlberg, L. (1999). The Cognitive development approach to moral education. In Ornstein, A.C. & Behar-Horenstein, L.S. (Eds.), *Contemporary issues in curriculum.* (pp. 163-175). Needham Heights, MA: Allyn & Bacon.

Kohlberg, L., Levine, C., & Hewer, A. (1983*). Moral stages: A current formulation and a response to critics*. New York, NY: Basal.

Kohn, A. (1993). *Punished by rewards: The trouble with gold stars, incentive plans, As, praise, and other bribes.* New York, NY: Houghton Mifflin.

Kozol, J. (1991). *Savage inequalities: Children in America's schools*. New York, NY: Harper Perennial.

Junger, S. (2016) *Tribe: On homecoming and belonging*. New York, NY: Hachette Book Group. Enjoyable psychoanalysis of community building concepts.

Ladson-BIllings, G. (1994). *The Dreamkeepers: Successful teachers of African American children*. San Francisco, CA: Jossey-Bass.

Lamotte, A. (1994). *Bird by bird: Some instructions on writing and life.* New York and Canada simultaneously, apparently: Random House.

McCourt, F. (2005). *Teacher man.* New York, NY: Scribner.

McCourt, F. (1996). *Angela's Ashes.* New York, NY: Scribner.

McIntosh, P. (1989/2003). White privilege: Unpacking the invisible knapsack. In S. Plous (Ed.), *Understanding prejudice and discrimination* (pp. 191-196). New York, NY, US: McGraw-Hill. Super-easy read with profound impact.

Marzano, R.J., Pickering, D.J. & Pollock, J.E. (2012). *Classroom instruction that works: Research-based strategies for increasing student achievement*. London, UK: Pearson.

Ness, M. (2001). Lessons of a first-year teacher. *Phi Delta Kappan*. 82 (9); 700-701.

Oakes, J. A. (1985). *Keeping track: How schools structure inequality.* New Haven, CN: Yale University Press.

Sedaris, D. (2008). *When you're engulfed in flames.* New York, NY: Little, Brown and Company.

Smith, D.L & Smith, B.S. (2016). Paperwork, meetings, and program review: The Challenges of university teaching in the 21st Century. In (Ed. E. Wright) W*hat to Expect and How to Respond: Distress and Success in Academia*. New York, NY: Rowman & Littlefield (p. 53-64). This chapter is probably why I didn't want to add a large section on leadership to the text. I already said it and try not to be repetitive.

Solorzano, D. G., & Bernal, D. D. (2001). Examining transformational resistance through a critical race and LatCrit theory framework: Chicana and Chicano students in an urban context. *Urban Education*. 36(3):308-342.

Steinem, G. (2016). *My life on the road.* New York, NY: Random House.

Strogatz, S. (2013). *The joy of X: A guided tour of math from one to infinity.* Boston, MA: Mariner Books.

Tovani, C. (2004). *Do I Really Have to Teach Reading?: Content Comprehension, Grades 6-12.* Stenhouse Publishers. My second textbook, after starting with Vacca and Vacca. I wanted to hear the author's voice and take a more pragmatic approach to literacy and this book fit that for years. It is a great read to understand the basics of one teacher's approach to content literacy. I learned to practice in the K-12 classroom from time-to-time through her example.

Truss, L. (2003). *Eats, shoots & leaves: The zero tolerance approach to punctuation.* New York, NY: Penguin Random House. I love that my computer tries to auto-correct her title to add a dash between zero and tolerance. Does Truss or Microsoft win that battle for you?

Turkle, S. (2015). *Reclaiming conversation: The power of talk in a digital age.* New York, NY: Penguin Press.

Vaca, R. & Vaca, J.A. (2016). *Content Area Reading: Literacy and Learning Across the Curriculum.* Boston, MA: Pearson.

Westover, T. (2018). *Educated.* New York, NY: Random House.

Vygotsky, L. S. (1978). *Mind in society: The development of higher psychological processes.* Cambridge, MA: Harvard University Press.

Zollman, A. (2011). Write is right: Using graphic organizers to improve mathematical problem solving. In Reeder, S. L., (Ed.) *Proceedings of the 38th Annual Meeting of the Research Council on Mathematics Learning.* (pp. 76-83). Cincinnati, OH: RCML.

THE END. For now.

Acknowledgements

Thanks so much to my husband and sons for the inspiration to write. I thank Helen Raica-Klotz as a reader and trusted feedback-provider, and my students, colleagues and community who I learn from each day. I thank Mrs. Jones who admired my poem on "Fang", the white German Shepherd who protected me from birth until age sixteen. Fang was a legend and anyone who understood made a connection with me. I thank the psychology teacher who let us write about our own serial killer. I read *Helter Skelter* about Charles Manson and analyzed the psychosis of those distant unknowns while ignoring the crazy that surrounds us all. I thank Drs. Bow-Tie, Ndura, and Hernandez for teaching the story as a forum for lessons. I thank Mary Harthun for leading the original cadre and teaching me to be a reflective action-researcher in addition to teacher. And, of course, I thank mom and dad and family.

After them, I thank these authors and so many more:

Frank McCourt, Jon Greene, David Sedaris, Amy Tan, Elizabeth Gilbert, Stephen King, Anne Lamotte, Mary Karr, etc. I love their books on how to be a writer and am fascinated by other people's lives and observational abilities.

I thank the late-night quiet when the sounds of war from down the stairs are tucked into bed and the only stirrings are the snores of the hounds. The time when the moon can talk with the stars and mortals can hear the songs. I thank the early-morning red-sky of sailors' warning and the dusk of bats and long-shadows and sunset walks if one is in the right locale. The hot sun of mid-day also deserves thanks as the heat burns away the moisture and waves crashing on the shore roar nature's roar. I thank the seasons and the experiences that make life a series of lessons. Many thanks to the wolves who howl at the moon and the community that continues to make me feel valued and loved. Thank you.

About the Author:

D.L. Smith lives with her two dogs and her two boys and her one husband in the quaint town of Frankenmuth where she enjoys writing, walking the dogs, and being the ball-girl for the Varsity soccer games. She is a literacy professor at Saginaw Valley State University and helps prepare new teachers to find their own path in the classroom.

Made in the USA
Monee, IL
23 January 2023

25912980R10148